Rethinking Student Discipline

Series Editors:
John T. Greer
Donn W. Gresso

Principals Taking
ACTION
Series

A joint publication of
THE NATIONAL ASSOCIATION OF SECONDARY SCHOOL PRINCIPALS
and
CORWIN PRESS, INC.

Rethinking Student Discipline
Alternatives That Work
   Paula M. Short, Rick Jay Short, and Charlie Blanton

Thriving on Stress for Success
   Walter H. Gmelch and Wilbert Chan

Paula M. Short
Rick Jay Short
Charlie Blanton

Rethinking Student Discipline

Alternatives That Work

CORWIN PRESS, INC.
A Sage Publications Company
Thousand Oaks, California

For information address:

Corwin Press, Inc.
A Sage Publications Company
2455 Teller Road
Thousand Oaks, California 91320

SAGE Publications Ltd.
6 Bonhill Street
London EC2A 4PU
United Kingdom

SAGE Publications India Pvt. Ltd.
M-32 Market
Greater Kailash I
New Delhi 110 048 India

Printed in the United States of America

Library of Congress Cataloging-in-Publication Data

Short, Paula M.
    Rethinking student discipline: alternatives that work / Paula M.
Short, Rick Jay Short, Charlie Blanton.
        p.   cm. — (Principals taking action)
    Includes bibliographical references and index.
    ISBN 0-8039-6084-0. — ISBN 0-8039-6085-9 (pbk.)
    1. School discipline—United States. 2. Classroom management—
United States. I. Short, Rick Jay II. Blanton, Charlie
III. Title. IV. Series.
LB3012.S54 1994   93-23415
371.5'0973—dc20   CIP

    95 96 97 10 9 8 7 6 5 4 3 2

Corwin Press Production Editor: Rebecca Holland

Contents

List of Figures

List of Tables

Preface

Administrators typically spend a great deal of time struggling
with student discipline problems. Many teachers express
frustration over the energy they expend controlling students in
the classroom—time and energy that could be used for instruction. The issue becomes even more complex when students with
special problems are thrown into the mix. Yet the most critical role
of the school administrator is to establish a school environment
supportive of good student behavior. How to go about achieving
this goal remains a difficult challenge for educators.

This book does what other publications on discipline do not
do. It provides an organizational look at building good school
discipline based on actual experiences in school settings. In addition, this book helps principals understand discipline and at-risk
populations, an area of great concern for educators. It also provides examples that give the administrator "hands on" material
for reframing the school's approach to discipline.

The strategies and methods discussed in the seven chapters of
the book are based on our years of practice and application and
that of others who have discovered useful ways of tackling the

discipline issue. It also draws from school discipline research. The examples and cases are actual insights from the authors' experiences and serve to illustrate and highlight the "reality" base for our approaches.

Chapter 1, "Introduction: Toward the Development of Self-Discipline," discusses the impact of teacher and administrator perceptions on how students learn to be self-disciplined. Here we present a fresh approach to thinking about developing student self-discipline as a critical means of addressing school discipline. We also suggest that discipline can be approached both from a schoolwide perspective as well as from the more traditional classroom view.

Chapter 2, "The Foundation: A Schoolwide Discipline Program," examines various approaches to discipline from a schoolwide perspective. The results of planning and developing a schoolwide plan for discipline are illustrated in the case study of Woolover High School. In discussing in- and out-of-school suspension, our view of in-school suspension is focused squarely on a model that helps students improve their behavior. In addition, we argue that the in-school suspension program must be one facet of a larger schoolwide plan to address student behavior. Our case studies illustrate clearly the outcomes of approaches based on various models employed.

Chapter 3, "Effective Building Blocks: In-Class Discipline," discusses various in-class strategies for good student discipline and the powerful influence of teacher perceptions about how students learn to behave. These strategies illustrate how contextual this issue remains and why principals need to recognize this influence in working with teachers on classroom discipline. Assertive discipline is also presented as an example of an effective classroom discipline strategy.

More and more teachers and administrators are forming problem-solving teams in order to make better decisions in schools. They are reframing discipline as an issue to be addressed through these school-level decision-making teams. Chapter 4, "When Something Extra Is Required: Problem-Solving Teams," examines practical considerations for building problem-solving teams and training participants for successful team outcomes. In addition, we describe an effective team problem-solving process that has been field-tested in schools.

Books on school discipline rarely address student behavior and the at-risk youth. Further, rarely do books focus on the debate on corporal punishment in schools. Chapters 5 and 6 tackle these difficult issues. Chapter 5, "Special Concerns: Discipline Strategies for Students At-Risk," provides a substantive discussion of the limitations of traditional discipline strategies for at-risk students. However, possibilities for successful programs for these students are provided in the section in school/community programs for at-risk youth. Chapter 6, "What About Corporal Punishment?," presents a cost-benefits analysis of corporal punishment to guide principals in reflecting on its use in schools. In addition, we suggest a number of alternatives to corporal punishment that, from our own experience, can be effective.

Finally, in Chapter 7, we reflect on some of the contradictions in considering school discipline. The "punishment" mentality so prevalent in schools today is challenged and more effective means to building good student behavior in secondary schools are discussed.

It is our sincere wish that this book will provide administrators with suggestions that guide, inform, help, and challenge. We believe that it provides a practical approach to discipline supported by research and extensive experience.

Paula M. Short
The Pennsylvania State University
Rick Jay Short
The American Psychological Association
Charlie Blanton
Partners in Profound Knowledge

About the Authors

Paula M. Short, Ph.D., is Associate Professor of Educational Administration at The Pennsylvania State University. Prior to joining higher education, she was a school and district administrator as well as program consultant in the North Carolina Department of Public Instruction. She has published widely in *Educational Administration Quarterly, Educational and Psychological Measurement, Journal of Research and Development in Education, Educational Research Quarterly, Planning and Changing,* and *NASSP Bulletin.* She assumed the editorship of the *Journal of School Leadership* in June, 1993; is a member of the editorial board of *Educational Administration Quarterly;* and is a correspondent for *Design for Leadership,* the publication of the National Policy Board for Educational Administration. She trains administrative assessors nationally for the National Association of Secondary School Principals. She is coauthor of *School Principals and Change* as well as coauthor of three book chapters in forthcoming books including *Principal as Instructional Leader* and *Restructuring Schools: Lessons From Ongoing Efforts* (Corwin Press). She codirected the three-year Empowered School District Project funded by the Danforth Foundation. She is president-elect of the National Council of Professors of Educational Administration, president of the Southern Regional Council for Educational Administration, and faculty associate in the University Council for Educational Administration.

Rick Jay Short, Ph.D., is Assistant Executive Director for Education, The American Psychological Association. He formerly was Associate Professor of School Psychology at The Pennsylvania State University. Prior to entering higher education, he worked extensively with troubled children and adolescents in residential treatment facilities, psychiatric hospitals, and private practice. A licensed psychologist and certified school psychologist, he has served as clinical director of a maximum security facility for delinquents and has worked as a school psychologist. He has published articles on psychological services for children and adolescents in such journals as *Professional Psychology: Research and Practice, Professional School Psychology, Psychology in the Schools, Educational and Psychological Measurement, Educational Research Quarterly, Topics in Early Childhood Special Education, Adolescence,* and *The High School Journal.* In addition, he has published several book chapters on prevention of substance abuse and delinquency. He is a member of the editorial board of *School Psychology Review,* and is serving as guest editor of a theme issue on conduct disorders for that journal. He also has authored and directed a number of federally funded grant projects for serving delinquent, at-risk, and substance-abusing children and adolescents. He has consulted with many school systems, universities, and public agencies on prevention of and intervention for substance abuse, delinquency, and risk factors in children and adolescents.

Charlie Blanton, Ph.D., is Consultant for Partners in Profound Knowledge Resource in Dallas, Texas. He conducts training in total quality management in organizations and companies across the country. Prior to joining PKR, he was principal of Newman Smith Senior High School in Carrollton, Texas, for eight years. During his administration the school was selected to participate in the Empowered School District Project funded by the Danforth Foundation. He also served as principal in the Dallas Independent

School District. He is Adjunct Professor of Educational Administration at Texas Woman's University where he teaches courses in planning. He has worked closely with the Texas Association for Supervision and Curriculum Development, the Texas Association for Secondary School Principals, and the National Association of Secondary School Principals. He regularly presents at the Association for Total Quality.

Introduction

Toward the Development of Self-Discipline

As former teachers, administrators, and school psychologist collectively, we have handled student discipline problems for many years. The continual struggle to understand how to make schools more positive environments gives us many sleepless nights. Why? Because we know that discipline, particularly as conceptualized in the school setting, is often associated with frustration for principals and teachers and negative feelings among students. Historically, schools were founded on an authoritarian model (which is still alive and well today) that promotes a punitive approach to discipline and produces little self-discipline. We would like to suggest an alternative view of discipline. Our view incorporates a balance between punishment and positive reinforcement that promotes the development of self-discipline or the use of appropriate behavior in a given situation. Outrageous thinking, you say! Read on.

Our thinking on discipline can be grouped under five general areas:

1. Schoolwide strategies and techniques that work to solve discipline problems;
2. Classroom management techniques that foster good discipline: clearly stated rules, supervision of student work, and responsiveness to student concerns;
3. Singular solutions to discipline problems, such as behavior modification, assertive discipline, and many others;
4. The variables that explain why certain schools have fewer discipline problems than others, such as the leadership of the principal and parental involvement;
5. The types of misbehavior of students and the characteristics of potentially disruptive students.

Our experience has been that methods of control in the schools are generally punitive. Those approaches, whether reward or punishment, tend to treat discipline as though it were simply a matter of employing techniques to control behavior. Next to verbal chastisement, supervision (in some form) is probably the most frequently used punishment in schools.

Approaching Discipline Along a Continuum of Practice

We prefer to look at discipline on the basis of three discipline models described by Wolfgang and Glickman (1980). This continuum ranges from child-centered to teacher-directed approaches. These three models are: relationship/listening; confronting/contracting; and rules reward and punishment.

The relationship/listening model assumes that students are rational and that the teacher must use minimum power in response to students. This is a therapeutic relationship, void of punishment, whereby supportive listening and observation techniques are utilized. The confronting/contracting model also is based on a nonpunitive relationship but the teacher openly confronts the student with the misbehavior, asking the student to cognitively reflect on the misbehavior and pushes the student for a contract or agreement on how the student will change behavior. The establishment of rules for acceptable behavior constitutes the third model area. We see this most regularly in our work with schools. Negative reinforcement, isolation, paddling, or other corporal punishment is used to enforce rules.

What Studies of Discipline Reveal

An exploratory study conducted in three school districts in the San Francisco-Oakland Bay area identified the major incidents of actual or potential student conflict observed by principals and vice principals in the area schools. Those incidents of conflict were:

- Tardiness
- Cutting class
- Spontaneous fighting
- Disrespect for teachers
- Disruptive school behavior
- Personal rivalries
- Extortion
- Theft
- Racial tensions
- Unprovoked assaults (Reed, 1983, p. 76)

Principals and vice principals in the study felt that schools must be supportive of students if conflict and disruptive behaviors were to be dealt with effectively. In all the sample schools in the study, students had the opportunity to defend their actions when they were involved in a conflict. Further, the principals felt that teachers and administrators who were sensitive, fair, and who had high standards and good rapport with students were most able to work with disruptive students. We, too, believe these qualities are vital.

Reasons for school conflict, according to the San Francisco-Bay Area study, were:

- Lack of parental control in the home
- Single parent families
- Low expectations of students on the part of teachers
- Impersonality of the school
- Racism
- Inflexibility and insensitivity of teachers
- Influence of television
- Neighborhood and community problems
- Values differences (Reed, 1983, p. 77)

When the principals and vice principals in the study were asked what policy on discipline they would like to implement in their school, they expressed little overall agreement. Individual responses included:

- Hire more full-time counselors to make home visits
- Have staff development on problem solving for conflict situations
- Select staff and remove ineffective teachers
- Get teachers more involved with students
- Encourage students to talk about problems before they erupt (Reed, 1983, p. 78)

Overall, the study indicates that problems of student conflict can be reduced when teachers are sensitive to student needs, when there is active- positive parent and community participation in the school, and when the school climate is such that respect is fostered for students, parents, and teachers.

Another study helpful to administrators is a synthesis of research on discipline by the Phi Delta Kappan Center for Evaluation, Development, and Research (1981). We found that the Kappan work substantiates the Bay Area studies. This synthesis supports our belief that when parents and teachers view students as able, valuable, and responsible, and invite them to behave accordingly, it is not surprising that students accept the invitation and exhibit self-discipline. Self-discipline is nurtured each time a parent or teacher treats a student with dignity, respect, and civility, all within a framework of positive expectations.

Techniques Alone Are Not the Answer

We do have serious concerns about a single focus on techniques. Techniques are important. They provide concrete actions to deal with specific problem behaviors. However, focusing on discipline techniques neglects the importance of the people who are responsible for using them. Administrators and teachers choose the way they respond to discipline problems. Their expectations, beliefs, and previous experience influence their choices. Characteristics of their role and the organization in which they work place constraints on their choices. Personal and organizational characteristics therefore may be at least as important to school discipline as specific discipline techniques. Even though these characteristics may influence the success or failure of such techniques, they have often received less attention than the techniques themselves.

Our contention is that conceiving of discipline as an organizational issue may enhance understanding of discipline problems. By conceptualizing student and teacher behavior as facets of the school milieu, administrators may be able to discover additional causes for and solutions to misbehavior.

Emphasizing technique, we firmly believe, is a narrow and potentially dangerous solution for school discipline. Whenever problem solvers restrict themselves to a single type of solution, they may become relatively insensitive to feedback concerning the effectiveness of that solution. When techniques fail, and we know that they sometimes do, educators often simply intensify their efforts, or they look for another, similar technique. By replacing unsuccessful techniques with new techniques, other potential problems and solutions within the school environment are ignored.

For example, the discipline problem may have been misdiagnosed. Individual teachers and students have often borne primary responsibility for classroom difficulties. We have seen discipline planners aim their efforts at changing or excluding members of these groups. Their solutions to discipline concerns have often included providing additional training in discipline techniques for teachers or tightening controls on problem students. These solutions implicitly identify teachers or students as problems, and technique as the solution. We have seen simplistic analysis of characteristics and needs of individual schools, resulting in little real change in the level of discipline problems.

Teachers, the frontline handlers of classroom discipline, bear most of the responsibility for smoothly running classes. Until recently, however, writers have seemed most interested in teachers as users of discipline strategies. Although undeniably important, we know that discipline techniques do not implement themselves. Teachers determine whether and how they use discipline techniques, determined in part by their beliefs about the way children should behave and be taught.

Importance of the Teacher's Discipline Philosophy

Our work in schools has suggested to us that there is a relationship between teacher discipline philosophy and school discipline. Willower's (1975) framework for teacher discipline philosophy is helpful in understanding this relationship. Willower found that educators vary along a continuum of beliefs about the way children learn to behave. We, too, have seen this in action. At one extreme of the continuum, custodial educators seem to emphasize classroom organization and structure. They believe that students are relatively passive receptacles of knowledge who learn best when there is a clear payoff for learning. Custodial educators believe that students must learn to conform to the system. They therefore emphasize routine and standardization, minimizing accommodation to individual differences in children. At the other extreme, humanistic educators emphasize the individual student. Humanistic educators believe that students are by nature active, positive, intrinsically motivated learners. They are comfortable with much activity and allow students to make choices concerning their educational activities. They minimize routine, bend rules, and view children as unique and active problem solvers. Sound familiar?

Differing Perceptions of Discipline Problems

Teachers with different discipline philosophies also differ in their identification of problem behaviors and their choice of strategies to deal with them (Glickman & Tamashiro, 1980; Short & Short, 1985a). Custodial educators identify a wide variety of behaviors as being problematic. They favor handling problem behaviors with control techniques such as punishment and suspension. In contrast, humanistic educators identify fewer types of behavior as being problematic. They believe that, given the right conditions, students want to and can improve their own behavior. Thus, discipline philosophy may determine perception of discipline problems as well as acceptability of discipline techniques in the classroom. Behaviors and techniques that are consistent with an educator's views about discipline may get more attention and action than those that are inconsistent with beliefs.

At the school level, the match between discipline philosophy and strategy may be crucial (Short & Short, 1985b). In fact, discipline models or strategies that are congruent with teachers' beliefs may be more widely used and effectively carried out than are counterbelief strategies. Also, teachers and administrators with whom we have worked are more committed to the successful implementation of interventions that are compatible with their beliefs. On the other hand, counterbelief strategies may result in increased conflict, a lower level of implementation, and decreased involvement in organizational efforts.

At any school, a range of discipline beliefs among teachers is likely to exist. Without awareness and accommodation of these belief differences, discipline planners risk ineffective or incomplete implementation of discipline programs. The inflexible mandate (which we have seen in many schools) for using any one model or strategy of discipline on a schoolwide basis may be inefficient and counterproductive. Such an implementation will probably be congruent with the philosophy of only a fraction of teachers in the school. Failure to attend to the philosophy variable in planning discipline may result in limited implementation of strategies and dissatisfaction of a percentage of implementers. We have seen these difficulties occur regardless of the demonstrated effectiveness of the particular strategy chosen for implementation.

Importance of School Climate

Our friend, Bill Wayson, found that more of the disruptive behavior that occurs in schools can be tied to poor school climate conditions rather than problems within students. He further reported that depersonalization among students and staff may be a major cause of discipline problems in schools. Students who leave school before graduation suffer from feelings of alienation and lack of purpose while they are attending school (Ward, 1982).

We have found that school practices that heighten student and staff involvement may decrease the occurrence of discipline problems. Student participation in school activities strongly relate to student commitment to schools. Activities that increase status, visibility, recognition, and group cohesiveness may decrease student alienation. Students want to be a part of schools that solicit their involvement and input. Negative student behaviors seem to decrease in schools in which the faculty have created climates of student belongingness and involvement.

We have determined that faculty involvement and commitment to school goals may also relate to improved school discipline. Administrative decisions that lower teacher decision-making prerogatives concerning what they teach, how they teach, and when they teach may encourage alienation. The school organization may influence both student behavior and teacher coping skills.

From our own experiences, the administrator, in setting and pursuing goals for the school, largely determines the discipline structure of the school. The administrator's ability to initiate and maintain a structure of order in the school is critical to the establishment of a school climate conducive to learning (Wu, Pink, Crain, & Moles, 1982). We adamantly believe that several facets of administrator role and behavior influence the character and effectiveness of discipline in the school.

The Administrator as Teacher Backup

The principal's most effective role in school discipline may be as a facilitator of teacher-initiated discipline (Short & Short, 1987).

Principals of well-disciplined schools are aware of discipline problems in their school, but provide opportunities and support for teachers to handle them. When teachers ask for help with problems, these principals provide resources and mediation to get the problem solved. Even though they expect the teacher to handle routine problems, they are sensitive to difficult cases and will provide leadership in such cases. With this active support, teachers' handling of routine discipline incidents becomes more effective and independent. Thus, principals in well-disciplined schools support teachers in taking a leadership role in handling discipline problems.

When principals become heavily involved in routine discipline problems, they may quickly become overwhelmed with calls from parents, referrals, and procedures. With too much work and inadequate time, they may handle those problems in impersonal, bureaucratic ways. They may then be less able than teachers to consider mitigating circumstances or individual student characteristics. Principals deluged with routine discipline problems may have little time to investigate individual cases. They may then summarily administer rote consequences for widely disparate behaviors. Also, principals are less aware of and less personally involved with individual problem students than their teachers. The greater the principal's role in handling routine discipline problems, the more likely the problem will be handled impersonally via administrative rules. This we know! Administrative handling increases the likelihood that the incident will result in the suspension of the problem student (Wu, Pink, Crain, & Moles, 1982).

Conclusions

It is our belief that successful school discipline is achieved through framing discipline as an organizational issue. Understanding teacher and student behavior as part of a larger organizational context provides a better opportunity to identify causes of poor student discipline and to structure more effective means for dealing with the causes. Findings from research suggest that organizational factors may play an important role in creating environments conducive to good student behavior. In addition, teacher beliefs about how students learn—and learn to behave— may be a strong influence on choice of discipline strategies used in classrooms. Understanding these influences help the adminis- trator better frame plans for dealing with student discipline.

The Foundation

A Schoolwide Discipline Program

Our work in schools suggests that organizational factors may be more significant than classroom techniques in explaining and dealing with discipline. Others have noted this also. Wayson (1985) has reported that four or five discipline incidents may originate in organizational characteristics, including how we organize and run schools. Gottredson (1984) found that school organizational factors had a significant effect on delinquency rates. These factors included involving staff, students, and community in planning and implementing change, using information to identify weaknesses, and focusing resources on those weaknesses in making changes in the curriculum and discipline procedures. Such strategies proved more effective in reducing delinquency than a large-scale intervention project that included intensive tutoring and high-quality counseling services. To us, this is most important information.

Our work with school discipline suggests the need for the establishment of a climate for effective school discipline. To establish such a school climate, administrators must examine discipline from a total school perspective. Lordon (1983) states that "if the individual teachers are to have the best chance to be successful in the classroom they must be part of a school staff which, in concert with a wise principal, is committed to total school pupil management" (p. 58). We agree with Lordon that key questions must be addressed by schools in examining school climate:

- How committed is the staff to discipline outside the classroom?
- Are school policies clear to students?
- Are detrimental attitudes avoided?
- Are policies and approaches to dealing with discipline problems consistent?
- Are planning and supervision policies established?

Duties that many teachers consider peripheral are critical in establishing good control and order in the schools. Expectations must be clearly established and communicated to the students in the school. Rules, procedures, and policies should be carefully explained to students. There should be consistency in behavioral expectations both in and out of the classroom as well as among classrooms. If students know what the school expects of them— and what to expect when they do not follow those expectations— most of them will fall in line.

Lordon also categorizes detrimental attitudes that hinder any attempts at total school expectations for student behavior:

- The Tardiness Syndrome or the teacher who is always late to class and in starting class
- The "He's Not My Student" Syndrome or the teacher who ignores misbehavior of students
- The "I'll Keep a Low Profile" Syndrome or the teacher who is present in body but not in mind
- The "It's None of My Business" Syndrome or the teacher who tries to become an ally of the student by subtly telling the student, "I'll stick to my business, you stick to yours." (p. 59)

The crucial key to an effective total school discipline program is shared values among students, teachers, parents, and administrators about what is acceptable, appropriate behavior in the particular school setting. We have found that several organizational characteristics relate to climates that are conducive to good student behavior. These characteristics include having a commitment to a plan of action, attention to teacher and principal role, and indication of strong student involvement.

Plan of Action

A schoolwide emphasis on improvement of student behavior is necessary in rallying commitment of both students and faculty. It is critical also that an actual plan be developed for implementation of strategies for improving student behavior. Wynn (1981) found, as we have, that schools that had a plan of action for guiding decision making and student behavior were successful in establishing good behavior. We agree with Wayson (1985) that effectively disciplined schools maintain a total school effort toward improving school discipline.

Teacher Role

We firmly believe that teacher participation in planning and implementation of the plan is mandatory. More important, the teacher provides a critical variable in this total school effort through development and utilization of problem-solving skills.

Student Involvement

Involved students—students who are actively engaged and interested in classroom activities—stay on-task at a higher level than students less interested and involved (Short & Short, 1990). This phenomenon exists at the schoolwide level. Students who tend to drop out of school perceive little sense of belonging (Ward, 1982). In effectively disciplined schools, students perceive a sense of belonging, a feeling that they are recognized and rewarded for their efforts. Even alternative schools have been shown to better meet student needs than regular schools in three areas: self-esteem, social, and self-actualization (Gregory & Smith, 1983).

Principal Behavior

A key principal behavior in a well-disciplined school is visibility. These principals expect teachers to solve their own classroom discipline problems and to resort to referral only if all else fails. Their key role is to facilitate the problem solving among school participants that results in collaborative approaches to establishing a positive school environment with clear expectations for students (Krajewski, 1977).

A Schoolwide Approach

Our experience in working with improving student discipline indicates that a schoolwide approach to discipline must focus on the commitment and support of the entire school faculty and staff in planning and implementation. Seven components are critical to the program: (a) development and utilization of teacher problem-solving skills in handling student problems; (b) student involvement in the development of schoolwide expectations for behavior; (c) public reinforcement for good behavior; (d) systematic approach to consistent use of consequences for not fulfilling expectations; (e) community involvement in the area of discipline; (f) schoolwide focus on establishing good behavior; and (g) use of data on discipline for evaluation and planning.

To illustrate, we will describe our work in helping a school implement a schoolwide discipline program. The school in this case implemented the Discipline Management Program (DMP) at the beginning of the 1986-1987 school year. In the year prior to implementation of the DMP, the principal and teachers told us that they had lost control. The principal spent much of the day handling referrals to the office for a number of incidents. Teachers spent most of the classroom time dealing with students who would not work and who were disrespectful. The general climate in the school was negative and stressful. Over 400 referrals were made to the principal during that year.

A Case in Point:
Woolover High School

The school we worked with was a 7-12 secondary school on the outskirts of a large midwestern metropolitan area. The student population was drawn from two distinct community groups: affluent families living around a large lake area and blue-collar families living near the school. Of the 30 faculty members, only one faculty member was new to the school at the time of the intervention. The school's principal had joined the school the previous year, thus serving as principal during both years reported in this study. There was no assistant principal in the school, but teachers served in some supervisory roles.

At the beginning of the study, the principal and teachers agreed that discipline would be a major focus for the school year, 1986-1987. Initial meetings occurred during in-service days at the beginning of the school year. Teachers discussed among themselves various concerns and agreed that discipline was the major issue. The principal, although prepared to go with any faculty decision, was pleased that improvement of discipline was chosen.

Subsequent discussions over the following two days resulted in the adoption of the Discipline Management Program. The DMP implementation was to proceed as follows:

1. Students were to be involved the first day of school in the development of schoolwide behavioral expectations.
2. Students were to be tested orally for their knowledge and understanding of expectations and consequences for not following expectations.
3. Faculty were to develop a classroom management process that involved a systematic way for the teacher to handle discipline problems—a type of assertive discipline but with a step process that required teacher problem solving and contact with parents.

4. Faculty would commit to consistent use of consequences schoolwide for failure to follow school expectations for behavior.

5. A questionnaire would be sent to parents to assess community/parental perceptions relative to community/parental responsibility for student behavior, type of consequences deemed for various infractions, and appropriate level of enforcement.

6. Teacher training in problem solving would occur.

7. Rewards in the form of movies and popcorn would be made monthly for those students without discipline referrals.

8. Collection and dissemination of monthly referral data would be provided to all faculty.

9. Systematic reinforcement of school expectations by the principal and teachers would occur through weekly discussions relative to student and faculty perceptions of how things were going.

10. End-of-year assessment of the Discipline Management Plan would be conducted by faculty.

The faculty met for 5 minutes every other day the first week of school to discuss how things were going. Students were given an oral test on school expectations and procedures at the end of each quarter. At a school assembly at the end of the first day of school the principal thanked the students for being involved in developing expectations, saying that they "made better rules than we (faculty) could have done" (Short & Clark, 1988).

Following the implementation of the DMP, referrals dropped from 454 to 60. Referrals for fighting dropped from 28 to 14. The number of referrals for disrespect to teachers fell from 62 to 35 with office referrals for disruptive noise falling from 338 to 5.

The findings from this school's efforts provide some empirical support for a total school approach for addressing school discipline problems. The discipline problems in this school were framed as organizationwide problems and, as such, in need of schoolwide strategies to address the issues. Although it is impossible to tease out which elements of the program contributed most directly to the program success, interviews with faculty and principal suggest that the total approach, including highlighting faculty and student ownership of both the problem and program, systematic attention of the principal, teacher training and involvement in problem solving with students, and consensus of focus for the program, was perceived to be the central ingredient. Interviews held with teachers indicated that they viewed their involvement in handling routine discipline problems in the classroom as part of their professional responsibility. They told us that problem solving with students was necessary if causes for misbehavior were to be identified and addressed.

Principal leadership—providing constant attention to creating a positive school involvement—was evident in this study. The principal told us that the program required constant attention to get started but the results were worth all the effort. This seems to support the effective schools research concerning the correlations between effective schools and principal leadership (Brookover & Lezotte, 1979; Edmonds, 1979).

In- and Out-of-School Suspension

Alternatives to out-of-school suspension that keep students in school can be varied. Those most often seen in schools are peer tutoring, time-out rooms, guidance centers, alternative learning centers, and in-school suspension (ISS) classrooms. The goal of any of these approaches should be to identify and remedy the problems and to help the students develop self-discipline.

To date it appears that the overriding goal of the implementation of ISS programs is to exclude the problem child from the regular classroom while continuing to provide some type of educational experience having the following characteristics:

1. Students are isolated while working on class assignments. There is no interaction with other suspended students or students in halls and cafeteria.
2. Students eat isolated from others in the cafeteria, mainly when the other students have gone.

3. Average length of assignment is 3 to 5 days.
4. Privileges are restricted and talking is not allowed.
5. Teachers send assignments to students to complete.

Although in-school suspension centers can differ greatly from school to school, in-school suspension programs appear to fall within three theoretical orientations (Garibaldi, 1978; Mendez & Sanders, 1981; Mizell, 1979; Pare, 1983; Short, 1988). We label these as punitive, therapeutic, and academic. Punitive programs, typically, expect the student to complete classwork, many times without help, while serving a required amount of punishment time. Dismissal may come earlier if the student shows "good behavior." This orientation implies that the problem is the student's. Rules are restrictive and inducement strategies are coercive.

Therapeutic orientations present a model that incorporates activities that help the student develop a better defined self-image, improve communication skills, participate in decision making, complete classwork concomitant with a "success" experience in academic work, and develop appropriate ways of dealing with the school environment. A variety of counseling approaches, including individual, group, and peer counseling, reality therapy, and referrals to outside counseling services, are utilized. Some programs encompass behavioral control components that focus on the student, teacher, parents, and school structure in attempting to identify strategies that could be used to fashion a program for a student. Programs of this type have activities in staff development, parent training, home and school survival training for students, and a time-out room (Short, 1988).

In-school suspension programs based on the theoretical orientation that discipline problems evolve from learning difficulties and the ensuing frustration place emphasis on basic skills in reading and writing, study habits, and other academic skills. A teacher gives individual instruction to students in need of it. The experience is structured with goal-oriented rules and regulations (Short, 1988).

Programs can be organized around one specific orientation, or may combine two or more theoretical orientations. The type of alternative educational experience provided seemingly is dependent on the theoretical orientation of the school implementing the suspension program.

We found that literature describing in-school suspension programs are written by individual administrators who generally feel that their particular programs are successful (Sykora, 1981). Though most of the articles cite success, we could find little statistical data that highlight what measures are being used in evaluating success. Few articles cite goals and objectives for programs other than the obvious reduction of out-of-school suspension.

We are concerned about the lack of parental involvement. Lordon (1983) has stressed the necessity for involvement of parents along with students, teachers, and administrators for a climate to be built in a school that fosters the development of self-discipline among its students.

Child advocates caution that in-school suspension must not become another tactic for discriminating against minority students of any type. We believe that administrators must be concerned about in-school alternatives to suspension that result only in students sitting in a room. Such alternatives are irresponsible management techniques that, over time, are not likely to help either the student or the school. In-school alternatives to suspension out-of-school must have as their purpose the identification and remedying of the problem while helping students develop self-discipline. This goes beyond mere punishment and control and involves the student, teacher, family, and community in an important problem-solving process.

Organizational Variables Influencing the Suspension of Students and School Discipline

In a study that analyzed national level data gathered for the Safe School Study, a number of relationships were explored to discover whether certain variables with the school organization influenced suspension of students. Suspension rates could best be predicted by knowing the kind of school a student went to and knowing how that school was run (Wu, Pink, Crain, & Moles,

1982). This research suggests that critical variables are teacher judgments and attitudes, school management and student governance practices, and racial, socioeconomic, and academic bias present in the school. In essence, the study suggested that, in addition to their behaviors, students' chances of being suspended increased if:

- Teachers are seen by students as relatively uninterested in them
- Teachers believe that students are incapable of solving problems
- Disciplinary matters are handled largely by administrative rules
- The school is not able to provide consistent and fair governance
- There is a relatively high degree of academic bias among school personnel
- There is a relatively high degree of racial bias present in the school (Wu, Pink, Crain, & Moles, 1982, p. 271)

Teacher Attitude

The chances of a student being suspended are not only affected by the teachers' personal interest in the student, but can be affected by the ways in which teachers perceive students; in particular, whether the teacher perceives students as capable of thinking through issues with logical reasoning. It is possible that teachers who think of students as being incapable of solving problems and thinking for themselves believe that the only solution to students with problems is to remove them from class. Our experience indicates that this is true because these teachers are likely to be less patient or less tolerant when students misbehave.

One particular study has been helpful in understanding how teacher attitude influences student discipline and how behavior is dealt with in schools. Metz (1978), in her field-based description of racial issues in two Ohio junior high schools, emphasized the importance of teacher philosophy, attitudes, and behaviors in the overall educational process. She described two particular teaching philosophies derived from observations and study of teachers in those schools. She found two specific patterns of teacher approaches to (a) the educational task and (b) classroom relations. Metz labeled these two philosophical stances "incorporative" and "developmental." In defining and describing the two approaches, she pointed out that the goals of the two approaches provide an idea of the teacher's understanding of the nature of children and of their appropriate role in the school. Thus, the incorporative philosophical position is described as follows:

> The teachers with incorporative goals generally use the child as an empty vessel, a small pitcher which must be filled with knowledge poured from the large pitcher of the adult. The child is more or less passive in this transaction, or more accurately, his actions and thoughts are of a standardized pattern activated by the directions of the teacher. (Metz, 1978, p. 48)

According to Metz, the incorporative teacher usually takes the present situation as given and makes very few changes. The teacher displays an attachment to routine and standardization while bemoaning the diversity found in children. Thus, the incorporative teacher tends not to reassess teaching methods based on student performance. Incorporative teachers tend to keep the same methods and goals even when children fail to respond. With classroom behavior or discipline, the incorporative teacher sets rules that are relatively unbendable. Circumstances surrounding an infraction are viewed as irrelevant to the rule and its enforcement. The incorporative teacher is the adult and, in effect, calls the shots because of position and age. The subordinate-superior relationship is the routine.

The developmental approach presents a contrast to the incorporative position as follows:

> The teachers with developmental goals generally consider the child to be inherently active and inherently curious about his environment. The task of the teacher then is not so much to fill the void of his ignorance as to channel his spontaneous curious activity in directions which will yield

the most useful harvest of facts, principles, and skills. (Metz, 1978, p. 48)

Metz quoted a teacher with the developmental philosophy as saying that "this body of knowledge has no meaning if you don't reach the prism that it's designed to enlighten. I have said before, and I'll say again and I think I'll always say, that I teach children" (1978, pp. 36-37). The developmental philosophy considers children as active rather than passive learners. Developmental teachers stress the better moments of children emphasizing their potential. They try to soften the limits imposed by the physical and social structures in the traditional school and classroom. Everything from scheduling to architecture is changed and rearranged to facilitate their efforts.

Developmental teachers acknowledge that there can be alternatives to situations. They grant that educational ends are open to interpretation in which students may share. These teachers take challenges to their directives that are seriously given as occasions for reevaluation as well as explanations of reasons for their plans.

Developmental teachers respond to the unique developmental characteristics of the early adolescent learner differently than the teacher holding the incorporative approach to instructional tasks and classroom behavior. Incorporative teachers operate with the expectation that students are passive receivers of the information espoused. They organize the learning experiences appropriate only to one developmental level, totally missing the developmental levels socially and intellectually of students above and below the one level. On the other hand, the teacher with a developmental philosophy-style will organize the learning tasks to meet the varying developmental levels in the class. Many methods, activities, and organizations will be employed in order to reach the student at the approach level of cognition development. The developmental teacher should be sensitive to both intraindividual and interindividual developmental differences and, by virtue of his or her teaching philosophy, will program for the class with these differences in mind. The incorporative teacher who maintains single-level programming will be unable to match accurately the instructional task with the adolescent learner.

The differences between developmental and incorporative teachers are not differences of technique but of philosophy, attitude, or style—their philosophy toward education in general. These attitudes underlie techniques, methods of teaching, and choice of techniques and methods of discipline.

School Management and Student Governance

Our experience as well as data from Safe School Study indicates that how the school is organized to handle discipline problems affects the rate of suspensions. We see a continuum that moves from schools where all disciplinary problems are dealt with by specific administrative rules to schools where a total school discipline philosophy utilizes everyone in developing and maintaining good discipline in the school setting. The Safe School Study suggests that more students have been suspended in schools where there is a high degree of administrative centralization in disciplinary matters (Wu, Pink, Crain, & Moles, 1982). We do not believe that this means that principals have no role at the opposite end of the continuum model. The establishment of a total school discipline program hinges on the involvement of the principal.

Wu, Pink, Crain, and Moles (1982) found that there was a negative correlation between good governance in a school and suspensions. We believe that good governance characteristics found in the Safe School Study were firm, fair, and consistent discipline practices.

Racial, Socioeconomic, and Academic Bias

The Safe School Study resulted in some troubling statistics. Males were more likely to be suspended than females. Blacks were twice as likely to be suspended than whites. Students whose fathers did not work or who received free lunch were more likely to be suspended than those who did not receive free lunch. Both school-level data and individual-level data showed that a student's chances of suspension were increased by a poor academic record or low-ability level. These are critical issues to us.

Critical Questions Schools Should Ask
About In-School Suspension

In our work with in-school suspension programs, we found it helpful to have school personnel address the following questions:

1. What does the school want the use of in-school suspension to accomplish? This question must be examined in light of the type of orientation—the process, structure, and personnel—that the in-school suspension program is to have.
2. Does the school have a total school discipline program? If the in-school suspension program is not a part of a total school discipline program, it may function only to segregate offenders. Schools must decide what in-school suspension is to accomplish in the total discipline program. The principal is the key in establishing the total program.
3. What are the prevailing teacher perceptions and philosophies in the school? An incorporative teaching philosophy appears to preclude any theoretical model except punitive.
4. Are schools attempting to identify the reasons for rules infractions and misbehaviors? There may well be more effective strategies for curbing incidents of class skipping, truancy, and many others. A school must look at the type of instructional program it offers. Does it encourage students to come to class?
5. Where are the positive reinforcers in the discipline program? Have schools defined discipline only in terms of punishment?
6. Students who get into trouble in schools are not all alike. There are the avoiders (class skipping, truancy, tardiness) and the disrupters (assaults, troublemaking, etc.). It is not a homogeneous group. Schools appear to be attempting to deal with every kind of student in the in-school suspension program. Would schools be more successful in changing student behaviors if they decided to deal with only one group—in particular, the most troublesome group of disrupters—by using in-school suspension and developing

other strategies for eradicating the class skipping, truancy, tardiness, and all other nonviolent disruption acts?

7. Is the standard practice of referring students for a specified period of time to in-school suspension contributing anything significant in changing the student's behavior? This encourages the "passive waiting out" of time.

8. Does the school use a valid measure of effectiveness in evaluating the in-school suspension program?

Dealing with school discipline problems has always been difficult. There are no easy solutions. The students who break rules, disrupt class, and assault others are complex as are the solutions to changing their behavior.

Two Comparative Case Studies

Case Study: Make Them Pay

This is the third year of existence for the in-school suspension program at this large senior high school. The school draws the 1,300 students from a high-income area and a more rural area. The modern school is situated outside the city limits. The facilities are fully equipped, with even the cafeteria enjoying a blue carpet that does not appear to show any wear after 5 years. Classrooms are clustered around teacher offices. The administration offices and guidance offices are spacious and nicely decorated. The school has a theater and a large modern media center.

The central office coordinator told us that the principal is responsible for developing the type of ISS program desired in the three high schools in the system. The principal at this particular school is the dominating figure in the school. A large portrait of this well-dressed African-American principal hangs in the administrative offices, given to the school by students several years ago. He has been in education 35 years. His faculty said that his style is supportive. He told us considerably about attempts to provide an instructional program that meets students' varied needs. The school has implemented a large variety of courses, attempting to help school become meaningful for all students. There is heavy instructional emphasis with teachers developing lesson plans based on curricula objectives. Those plans are reviewed by the assistant principals regularly.

Stated goals. The stated goals emphasize a punitive model, excluding troublemakers from the classroom while keeping them in school. The system-level administrator in charge of ISS told us that the goals of ISS were those listed in the project proposal: To provide guidance to behaviorally disruptive students and reduce the number of disciplinary suspensions and expulsions. He mentioned that a further purpose of ISS was to reduce the potential for crime by keeping kids off the streets, stating that police had noticed a difference in crime during the school day. He also said that the program could do counseling and remediation but that it wasn't needed. He does not feel that ISS requires a professional to "monitor" the program. The school administrator views the overriding goal as keeping the student in school while completing classwork. According to the ISS teacher, the main purpose of ISS is to keep kids off the street.

Actual goals. The program is punitive. True to the attitudes of the administration, it does not deal in remediation. What little counseling behavior that does occur is at the initiation of the ISS teacher who has some questions about being able to carry out a counseling program. He is looking for resources to help. The number of out-of-school suspensions decreased by 409 students during the first year of ISS. However, that number did not decrease the following year. Referrals to the assistant principal decreased from 412 during the first year of ISS to 211 for the second year (Table 2.1); a reflection, perhaps, as the principal stated, of the growing expectation that teachers who send students to an assistant principal are saying that they have done all that they could. Statistical information provided by the principal revealed the following:

The principal told us that the basic rule he follows in determining whether an out-of-school suspension or an in-school suspen-

TABLE 2.1 Discipline Data

Year before in-school suspension program		
Expulsions	0	
Suspensions	479	
Dropouts	71	
Court referrals	0	
First year of program		
Expulsions	0	No change
Suspensions	70	Decrease of 409 students
Dropouts	52	Decrease of 19 students
Court referrals	0	No change
Referrals to assistant principals	412	
Second year of program		
Expulsions	0	No change
Suspensions	70	No change
Dropouts	42	Decrease of 10 from 1980-81; decrease of 29 over base year
Court referrals	0	No change
Referrals to assistant principals	211	

sion is appropriate is whether the infraction disrupts others (out-of-school) or only disrupts the student. He cited being tardy or smoking in an inappropriate place as an example of disruption of self. Table 2.2 shows the school discipline code in the student handbook that outlines the following rules.

The assistant principals involve the guidance counselor when special help is needed with a referral. The counselors, however, are not directly involved in the in-school suspension program. The ISS teacher, a young coach and former security guard, indicates a need for counseling of students in ISS, based on his questions concerning resources that he might tap for help. He suggested to us that a weekly visit from a social worker would help.

TABLE 2.2 School Discipline Code

There will be times that a student will be sent home instead of being assigned to in-school suspension; this will be for more serious offenses such as:

Fighting, stealing, possession of the following drugs:

- Narcotics
- Marijuana
- Hallucinogenic drugs
- Amphetamines
- Barbiturates
- Alcoholic beverages
- Intoxicants of any kind

Skipping school:

- 1st offense—3 days in-school suspension
- 2nd offense—5 days in-school suspension
- 3rd offense—3 days suspension from school

Cafeteria:

- Students caught cutting lunch lines or leaving trays and utensils on the table will be assigned to in-school suspension for one day.
- A second offense, student will be assigned to in-school suspension for 3 days.

Leaving school without permission: Same as above, skipping school.

Class attendance: Students are required to attend all classes and study halls. If a student is absent from class or study hall, the teacher will send a report of this absence to the dean. Cutting of classes and study halls will not be tolerated and offenders will be disciplined. The penalty for cutting class is as follows:

- 1st offense—Warning
- 2nd offense—Assigned to in-school suspension not less than 3 days nor more than 5 days. Parents will be contacted by letter.
- 3rd offense—Suspended for 5 days in-school suspension. A parent conference will be required at school upon student's return to classes.
- 4th offense—Suspended 3 days from school. A parent conference is required before student is readmitted to school. (No phone calls.)

The ISS classroom, located in a shop area, is a large room with cement floors, high ceilings, and 30-odd desks spaciously arranged classroom-style with the teacher's desk at the front. There are many distractions—other students constantly moving in and out of an office off the room and the loud noise of an electric saw next door. The saw is so loud that one cannot hear anything else. The ISS teacher appears uncomfortable in his role. He tells us that he needs new ideas to improve. He feels that he is expected to counsel these students. He feels that it is not easy to counsel and be strict. He tells us he is bored. We see several students throw small wads of paper and create noises, which went unnoticed by the teacher.

There is the general feeling that the students referred to ISS are not necessarily the lower academic level students. One teacher told us that they really don't have any bad kids. With the large number of curriculum offerings, many designated for those needing some type of remedial help, those remedial-type students tend not to be in ISS. The principal strongly feels that there is no need for a remedial component in ISS for this reason.

Students in ISS are indeed in a restrictive environment. Rules explain that students will lose most privileges, be isolated from peers, and will complete all assignments from classes. One student told us that she had finished all assignments early but could not get any further assignments to complete because her teacher didn't want her to get ahead of the rest of the class. She said that she got a lot more work done here than in class. She said that she missed lectures and demonstrations, all of which hurt her work, especially in math. One teacher told us that students are allowed to leave ISS for a particular class movie, lecture, or other activity in which the class teacher feels the student must participate.

As part of normal school procedure, assistant principals do not make any decisions about referral to ISS prior to talking to the referring teachers, in order to get a clear understanding of what happened. The administration feels it is important not to spring new things on the kids without prior warning. Fairness is a word used often by the principal. No student is sent directly to ISS after a classroom incident. Cooling off is done in the assistant principal's office. Referred students enter ISS the day after the infraction. The administrator tells us that the overall school policy has been tightened up. There is a general feeling that teachers are firmer than in past years. Students complete all assignments submitted by teachers. Forms are provided to teachers as shown in Figure 2.1.

The punitive model evident in stated goals is in operation. The reduction of overall out-of-school suspensions appears to have been accomplished. Granted, the number of referrals decreased dramatically during the second year of existence, but it is difficult to say that ISS has been responsible for this occurrence. No observable counseling or behavioral guidance element appears to exist in the program. Students basically do their time and leave. Because the ISS teacher himself has some trouble with the behavior of referred students, it is debatable whether ISS is affecting disruptive behavior. Much of the effort in providing guidance appears to occur prior to referral. The administrative use of in-school suspension to enforce set rules and regulations is the dominating factor influencing the punitive model for the program. Except for this fact, there could possibly be a more therapeutic model in operation, as the faculty seem to be very responsive to student needs and to care about the students. They view students as capable of problem solving. Yet, the one variable the centralization of discipline process inhibits is the use of the therapeutic model.

Case Study: In-School Alternative Learning Center

This urban junior high school (75% black, 25% white) has recently adopted the middle school organizational pattern with its 500 sixth-, seventh-, and eighth-grade students grouped around teams of teachers for instructional and advising activities. The principal, a state leader in the middle school association, has "gently led" his faculty to adopt a more developmental approach to working with students. The entire faculty has participated in numerous staff development activities dealing with the characteristics of the middle school child, the adviser-advisee concept, and the implications of the middle school concept in instruction.

Personnel think that students are getting more personal attention and are feeling more secure. The principal has established the expectations that teachers will exercise patience and understanding

TO: _____

FROM: _____
     ISS

_____ is to report to ISS for _____ days beginning _____ .

REASON FOR ISS:	Fighting	_____	Skipping class	_____	Not following directions	_____
	Smoking	_____	Skipping all day	_____	Theft	_____
	Constant tardies	_____	Drugs & alcohol	_____	Disruptive class behavior	_____

Other: _____

Please indicate below the assignments you wish for this student to complete. Any special needs or concerns should be indicated. Please place assignments in my box in either _____ or _____ building by 7:45 a.m. on the morning that the student begins in ISS, or send materials directly to _____ in room _____ .

Day 1 _____

Day 2 _____

Day 3 _____

Day 4 _____

Day 5 _____

Figure 2.1. ISS Teacher Notification Memo

of students at this age level. The assistant principals to whom referrals from teachers are sent allow students to "tell their side of the story" and send referred students to the guidance counselor before any alternative placement. Because both parents of students generally work, parental pressure on the school is low.

Stated goals. School officials told us that the theoretical orientation of the in-school suspension program is a combination of academic (remedial) and punitive. The stated goals of the program are to cut down on suspension while providing a place for students who can't function in the average classroom. It is believed that the Alternative Learning Center (ALC) is a place for students who couldn't learn no matter what the problem. Administrators describe the program this year as being "more ISS" because many problems of a less severe nature are being resolved within the teams due to the middle school programs. The school principal states that the program is more than disciplinary; it serves to help the students academically.

The tone of the "Student Discipline Policy" (see Table 2.3) emphasizes the attainment of academic goals in an environment where students, who have responsibility for their behavior, behave in an acceptable manner. In line with the developmental educational philosophy, it states that there can be bad days.

Actual goals. The program combines a punitive and remedial orientation in its actual dealings with students. Though students are referred primarily for "disrespect and disobedience," strong efforts are directed toward working with the student's academic problems. One student learned to read during a long-term placement in ALC. In the more punitive sense students are isolated, are required to follow strict rules, and lose certain privileges.

The Alternative Learning Center has served many purposes during its 6 years of existence. The assistant principal for instruction will, at times, teach courses to entire classes of resource students. One year, science instruction for these students was carried out in ALC. Students have been assigned permanently to ALC where a great deal of remedial help exists. The ALC, though staffed by an aide, has developed a large amount of remedial materials that students often

TABLE 2.3 Student Discipline Policy

Discipline at our school is based on "facts of life" that are easily understood by students.

1. Your *main goal* in school is *education*, which is a thing worth having just for its own sake. It helps you learn more, faster. It prepares you for the demands of a job later in life.
2. So, any person preventing you, or himself, from reaching this goal is going to be disciplined. To learn the most you can requires being able to *listen, recite, share,* and *concentrate without interference.* This school will protect your right to an education without interference.
3. Like your home, there are authorities. At school these authorities have made it their business to learn about young people and the subjects they teach. *Their main goal is your welfare and education.* They care enough about you to keep after you so you will make it. If your teachers aren't all alike as far as rewards, punishment, discipline—you've learned a valuable fact of life. Teachers aren't all alike—and neither are the many people with whom you'll come in contact, now or later in life. You will have to *learn* to adjust to a variety of demands from a variety of personalities.

On the other hand —

1. No one is perfect—some of us have "bad days." Sometimes we are distracted. So what? What counts is a desire to improve behavior and show a changing attitude. A few mistakes will not be held against you.
2. School can be a pleasant experience—you get out of it exactly what you put into it.
3. Rules apply to all—no one is singled out for special treatment.

use when in ALC. The impetus for this emphasis has come from the assistant principal for instruction.

Parental involvement is evident. Parents are required to come to school for a conference before the student is allowed to return to class from the Alternative Learning Center.

Students work in a restricted environment, governed by rules and isolationism while completing class assignments. Some desks

TABLE 2.4 Alternative Learning Center (Fall Semester)

Reason for ALC placement	Number of 50-minute periods
Disciplinary	
Fighting or physical abuse	1,459
Disrespectfulness or verbal abuse	451
Disruptive behavior throughout the building or on the school bus	354
Failing to follow instructions of school personnel	328
Leaving school without permission	206
Profanity or obscene language	64
Damage to school or private property	48
Stealing or extortion	48
Nondisciplinary	
Other (various reasons)	26
English as a second language	140

are placed in cubbyholes along the walls for students to sit when they first enter ALC. As they exhibit observance of the rules, they may be advanced to sitting in desks placed in rows. Books of interest to students are on tables. Audiovisual materials such as stories on tapes are available. Files of worksheets, categorized by subject, are available for students to use. Students feel these materials help because many who are not in ALC come by to request materials to help them in their studies. Statistics illustrate periods spent in the Alternative Learning Center for various infractions as shown in Table 2.4.

The program appears to be functioning close to the goals it has set for itself. Its emphasis is heavy on the remedial orientation. The leadership of the school principal, emphasizing the developmental teaching philosophy, seems to have an important influence on the theoretical orientation of the in-school suspension program and the congruency between stated goals and actual operations of the program. Teachers and the principal talked to us about helping students develop self-discipline. The large amount of concern about helping students achieve academically at any ability level

TABLE 2.5 In-School Suspension Student Evaluation

1. Has in-school suspension benefited you in any way? Please explain.

2. Explain in detail some things that you like about in-school suspension.

3. What are some things that you disliked about in-school suspension?

4. Do you think the teacher was helpful? Explain.

5. What are some changes you would like to see made in in-school suspension to make it more effective for students and teachers?

Comments:

illustrates a lack of academic bias and suggests a genuine concern for finding strategies to help the low achiever. Students are requested to evaluate their stay in the Alternative Learning Center as shown in Table 2.5.

Teachers, in turn, are asked to assess the behavior of students as they return to classes. Follow-up forms used in this process are seen in Figure 2.2. Examples of student contracts often used are shown in Figure 2.3.

TO: _____

FROM: _____

I need an evaluation of _____'s progress for the past weeks. Please answer the following questions regarding his/her progress. Please return to my box as soon as possible.

1. Attendance: _____
2. Behavior: _____
3. Performance: _____
4. Participation: _____
5. Attitude: _____
6. Peer relationship: _____
7. Student-Teacher relationship: _____
8. Class grade at this time: _____
Comments or recommendations: _____

_____
(teacher's signature)

Figure 2.2. In-School Suspension Follow-Up

Date: _____

I, _____, have agreed to complete this contract each day for 5 days.
I will take this contract to _____ each day during _____ period lunch. My goal is to receive
points from each teacher daily. I realize that failure to do a contract and to receive acceptable scores will result in
my re-assignment to ISS.

Evaluation Code: 2-Good   1-Satisfactory   0-Needs Improvement

Periods	1	2	3	4	5	6	7	8
On time to class								
Completed and turned in homework								
Completed daily work on time								
Refrained from excessive talking and noise making								
Showed respect to teacher and cooperated in following directions								
Brought books, pencil, paper to class								
Did not argue with classmates								
Totals								
Teacher's Signature								

Teacher Comments (opt.) _____

Figure 2.3. Student Contract

Conclusions

The most effective approach to establishing an environment conducive to good student behavior is to develop a schoolwide plan for discipline. We know that a critical variable is the shared values among students, teachers, parents, and administrators about what is acceptable, appropriate behavior in a particular school setting. Central to a schoolwide discipline plan is a commitment to a plan, an understanding of roles of the teachers and principal, and strong student involvement in the functioning of the school. Woolover High School's Discipline Management Plan (DMP) illustrates how a focus by all faculty and students on a schoolwide plan can reduce drastically the need to refer students to the principal for discipline problems. The DMP also demonstrates the ability of a school to change the overall behavior of students in a positive climate supportive of good student behavior.

Effective Building Blocks

In-Class Discipline

As can be seen from reading previous chapters, we believe effective school discipline requires a schoolwide, or organizational, focus. However, classroom discipline is a basic component of organizational discipline programs and should receive considerable attention in overall discipline planning. In this chapter, we will discuss some important general issues in classroom discipline. We also will present some common elements of effective discipline programs and provide an example of one such program.

Teacher Beliefs and Expectations

As noted in Chapter 1, all teachers have beliefs about the kind of classroom in which they want to teach and the kind of student behaviors that they want to promote. However, teachers often vary widely in their expectations concerning student behavior and in the techniques they use to teach appropriate behavior. These expectations and techniques may be influenced by their beliefs about the way children should behave and the best interventions to promote such behavior (Short & Short, 1985b).

A recent study investigated the relationship of such teacher beliefs to number and type of reported problem behaviors and to preferences for classroom interventions (Short & Short, 1990). Teachers in the study completed the Pupil Control Ideology (PCI) form (Willower, Eidell, & Hoy, 1967) and a questionnaire concerning behavior problems in their classrooms and interventions that they use and find effective in dealing with these problems. Items on the questionnaire were adapted from a questionnaire developed by Moore and Cooper (1984). Problems in the questionnaire were:

- verbal impertinence or discourteousness toward the teacher
- throwing objects
- failure to do homework or other assignments
- cheating
- physical violence against the teacher
- using profane and obscene language
- destruction of school property
- fighting
- truancy
- physical violence against teachers other than yourself
- smoking in the building
- use of drugs
- gang fighting
- carrying dangerous weapons
- stealing

Interventions on the questionnaire were:

- extra assignments
- within-school suspension

- notes written to parents
- verbal reprimands
- corporal punishment
- suspension from school
- detention after school hours
- restrictions from extracurricular activities

Overall, teachers in the study reported failure to do homework, drug abuse, truancy, cheating, and verbal impertinence to be the most widespread discipline problems in their school. They reported using verbal reprimands, detentions, and notes to parents most often, and considered these discipline strategies to be the most effective available. However, custodial educators (as identified by the PCI) were more likely than humanistic teachers to identify some common classroom occurrences as being problematic. These included verbal impertinence and failure to complete assignments. They also considered truancy to be more troublesome than did their more humanistic colleagues. In contrast, humanistic educators viewed carrying dangerous weapons as being more problematic than did custodial educators.

Custodial educators, in their beliefs that students must learn to conform to organizational norms, may be more likely to perceive violations of those norms as behavior problems. In contrast, humanistic teachers may view such behaviors as manifestations of emotional concerns or a poor classroom/student match. Humanistic teachers also may consider such premeditated and potentially deadly behavior as carrying weapons to differ qualitatively from the previously mentioned classroom problems, whereas custodial teachers consider these behaviors to represent a single dimension. Humanistic educators used notes to parents more often and in-school suspension and detention less often than custodial educators, apparently favoring interventions involving communication and negotiation, such as parent contact. Custodial educators seemed to subscribe to more punitive or controlling strategies such as restrictions.

Thus, teacher beliefs may influence expectations, perception of classroom problems, and preference for intervention techniques in the classroom. Behaviors and techniques that are consistent with an educator's views about socialization may get more attention and action than those that are inconsistent with such beliefs. The match between these teacher beliefs, problem identification, and problem intervention may be crucial (Short & Short, 1990). Intervention models or strategies that are congruent with educator beliefs may be more widely used and effectively implemented than are counterbelief strategies. Also, educators may be more committed to the successful implementation of interventions that are compatible with their beliefs. On the other hand, counterbelief strategies may result in increased conflict, a lower level of implementation, and decreased involvement.

Diversity in Discipline Programs

Even a cursory examination of the literature on school discipline shows that numerous discipline programs and strategies have been proposed, often founded in widely divergent theoretical orientations and supported with varying levels of data on their effectiveness. As previously noted, the acceptability of these programs, as well as the types of problems to which they will be applied, may be determined by teacher characteristics more than objective effectiveness.

Because it is beyond the scope of this book to present this diversity of approaches, we have chosen to discuss a few common characteristics shared by most effective discipline programs. Regardless of the approach that a particular classroom institutes or the beliefs of the teacher, these characteristics should be prominent components of the program. These characteristics include clear expectations, consistent and balanced consequences, and student involvement.

Another study provides some initial support for the importance of these variables in maintaining students' task-oriented behavior (Short & Short, 1988). This study investigated the relationship of perceived classroom and teacher characteristics to student on-task behavior in secondary school classrooms. On-task behavior may be an important predictor of student achievement

(Bloom, 1968; Carroll, 1963; Good & Brophy, 1984). On-task behavior also seems relevant in maintaining classroom order, and recently has received national attention as an educationally malleable learning factor. In particular, classrooms that students perceive to be highly structured, organized, and rule-governed with a strong focus on task completion and teacher control should exhibit higher levels of on-task behavior. Perceived teacher characteristics of supportiveness, control, and innovation and the classroom characteristics of rule clarity were related significantly to observed on-task behavior in the classroom.

Expectations

Teachers convey their expectations for student behavior in the classroom in a number of ways. One such way is direct expression. Expressions of teacher approval or disapproval set up standards against which students judge their behavior. Another way is routine. Classroom routines convey a sense of what is expected in the classroom, as well as what is considered unusual or outside of normal procedure. Teacher expressions and classroom routines can be verbal or nonverbal, formal or informal, systematic or unsystematic, rigid or flexible. However, the way that these preferences are translated into expectations for classroom behavior often influences the extent to which such expectations are fulfilled.

Perhaps the most systematic and formal method for expressing expectations is the use of classroom rules. Most classrooms have rules to which students are expected to conform. Many classrooms have developed formal rules that are posted somewhere in the room. However, it is important to note that informal rules or expectations often complement, and sometimes negate, these formal classroom rules. An example of such a conflict is a formal rule against talking without permission in the classroom that is enforced only during some classes or with some students. Informal permission to talk during group time mediates the formal rule in allowing talking without permission in some situations. Although astute and rule-abiding students soon learn to reconcile these disparities, lack of rule clarity often interferes with classroom tasks (Short & Short, 1988).

Rules About Rules

Examination of almost any extant discipline program (e.g., behavior modification, assertive discipline, reality therapy) illustrates the central role of rules in a discipline program. In these and other programs, effective use of rules is a major component and an important strategy for structuring positive behavior and preventing negative behavior.

We have found that several general characteristics seem important to the effectiveness of classroom discipline rules. Although these characteristics are based on common sense, it is not uncommon to find at least some of them absent in classrooms. This suggests that they may not be as self-evident as they appear.

1. Rules should be relatively few in number. Most classrooms can be managed with as few as three or four rules.
2. Rules should be simple. Simple sentences should be used to aid understanding.
3. Rules should be stated positively. It is easier and more efficient to state positive expectations than it is to list all unacceptable behaviors.
4. Rules should be clear. Students should be able to recognize acceptable behavior from the rule, and students and teacher should be able to agree on distinctions between rule-abiding and rule-breaking behavior.
5. Rules should be fundamental. The teacher should include as rules only those expectations that are non-negotiable or that already have been negotiated.

Some examples of rules for the classroom include:

1. Always be on time.
2. Wait until you are called on to talk.
3. Complete your assignments.
4. Respect your teachers and classmates.

Consequences

Classroom rules certainly are an important component of any discipline program; however, rules by themselves serve as little more than behavioral ideals or guidelines. Absent contingencies for compliance and infraction, they often are forgotten, or worse, ignored. Used appropriately, consequences provide an essential medium for teaching self-monitoring and self-correction of behavior by students. With this in mind, several characteristics of effective consequences should be pointed out.

1. Consequences should be balanced; that is, contingencies should be just as available for compliance with classroom rules as they are for rule infractions. A typical error in formulating classroom discipline is to spend considerable time devising punishers for negative behavior without a concomitant concern for rewarding positive behavior. Such a strategy directs predictable teacher attention, a powerful reinforcer, to negative behaviors but not to positive behaviors. This may result in an increase in the very behaviors that the teacher seeks to discourage.

   As an example of this point, we have found that consistent rewards such as free time and group activities can increase observance of classroom rules. It is important, though, that students find these activities truly rewarding. This may require some flexibility and creativity on the part of the administrator and the teacher. Unfortunately, sometimes it may be difficult to find activities in the classroom that students will work for without getting bored with them. With a little thought and negotiation with the class, some desirable and practical options should become apparent. In a secondary crisis classroom in which one of us worked some years ago, the only thing that really kept the interest of the class was getting to leave school a few minutes early on Friday afternoons!

2. Consequences should be within ready control of the teacher. Consistency and follow-through are important characteristics

of any classroom intervention. When the teacher is consistent and thorough in his or her behavior, students learn that their own behavior has predictable consequences. Under these circumstances, they soon learn to modulate their behavior to obtain desirable outcomes. However, consistency and follow-through often are difficult to maintain when they require enforcing consequences that are inconvenient, disruptive, or beyond teacher control. Contingencies that are reasonably simple and unobtrusive probably will be used more systematically; therefore, they may be more effective teaching tools than complex or inaccessible options.

An excellent example of this point is Ms. Davis, a teacher with whom one of us worked a few years ago. Ms. Davis controlled her class by threats. Most of these threats were never executed, and many of them were obviously beyond the will and the capability of Ms. Davis to enforce. For example, she frequently threatened to detain offending students until 9:00 p.m.—even though both she and the students realized that that consequence was improbable. The threat was never carried out, and students soon learned to ignore it.

3. Consequences should be proportionate to and, if possible, logically linked with behaviors. Classroom discipline strategies may be characterized best as tools to teach acceptable school behaviors. Learning is easier and occurs more rapidly when associations are direct and understandable. For this reason, contingencies that somehow are related to particular behaviors may be easier to learn and enforce. An example of this connectedness is using break time to complete unfinished work. If a classroom rule is to complete work, then a functional consequence of failing to complete work could be to use time that normally would be used as free time to accomplish that task. In addition to being a less desirable outcome for the student, using free time to complete work reinforces the importance of work completion over unstructured use of time.

4. Consequences should be developed and understood by the class prior to their implementation. Although types of con-

sequences can be formulated broadly so that some latitude in specific actions is available, general consequences for positive and negative behavior should be predictable. Students may perceive unexpected strategies as being unfair and arbitrary or may be difficult to understand in association with student behavior. Again, actions that are easy to understand and predict are better teaching tools than unforeseeable or indirect options.

Again, Ms. Davis provides an example of this point. In the above situation, she finally became frustrated with the class and grabbed a paper of one of the students and tore it up. This certainly was punishing but the class considered it unfair, because it was unexpected and it didn't seem to fit the offense. As a result, her behavior actually increased negative behaviors.

Involvement

Even very young students often can play an active role in making decisions about acceptable classroom functioning. Student involvement in formulating and negotiating classroom rules and contingencies frequently increases their commitment to conforming with classroom expectations. In addition, such shared decision making can model effective group process skills and teach self-judgment in monitoring and evaluating behavior. In our experience, several points should be emphasized in enlisting student involvement in classroom discipline.

1. Final approval for all decisions rests with the teacher. Student group decisions about classroom functioning almost always concur with those of the teacher. However, occasional divergence in perceptions should be expected and discussed openly. Perhaps surprisingly, our experience has been that student groups differ from teachers most in two ways; they propose many more rules than their teachers, and they advocate harsher consequences for infractions than their teachers. Without appearing arbitrary, teachers should discuss disparate views with their class to arrive at some consensus or near-consensus about classroom order.

2. Input in making decisions about rules and contingencies does not extend to involvement in carrying out negative consequences. The class should understand clearly that the teacher is responsible for and comfortable with implementing contingencies for classroom behavior, particularly in the case of rule infractions. Unsupervised or unauthorized enforcement of negative contingencies may result in undesirable outcomes and may teach a lack of respect for classroom order.

3. Discussion about rules, expectations, and outcomes should be conducted formally during the first week or so of class, with refresher discussions scheduled periodically during the year. Early decision making about classroom structure encourages predictability and objective input about behavior. It avoids crisis management discussions that sometime occur in the absence of preplanned structure. Periodic review of initial structure allows for adjustment of wording or expectations, along with reaffirmation of original rules. Finally, this procedure establishes a consistent avenue for students to provide input, thus contributing to positive classroom structure.

Regardless of the particular model or program used in the classroom, effective classroom discipline programs integrate expectations, consequences, and involvement into a comprehensive program. This program provides a framework for dealing with almost any classroom behavior in a planned and predictable manner, and encourages the perception of the teacher as an organized, fair implementer of agreed-on procedures. We encourage you to inspect your own preferred discipline approach to compare it to the points made here. A representation of components of a comprehensive discipline program is presented in Figure 3.1.

An Example: Assertive Discipline

Although a large number of discipline approaches are available, one widely used discipline program will serve to illustrate the points made in this chapter. This approach is assertive disci-

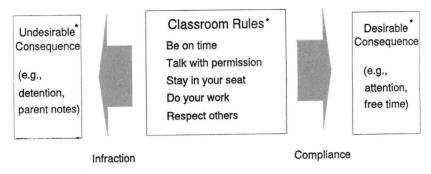

Infraction   Compliance

* Optimally, both teacher and students should be involved in negotiating these.

Figure 3.1. A Comprehensive Discipline Approach

pline (Canter & Canter, 1981). Assertive discipline is a competency-based approach to discipline developed by Lee Canter. It provides the skills and confidence teachers need to "take charge" in their classroom. Teachers must use a systematic approach to discipline that enables them to set firm consistent limits for the students. Assertive discipline allows teachers to put aside yelling and threatening, offering instead a positive power that prevents their giving in or giving up. Canter's key ideas illustrate its philosophy.

Key Idea #1

Teachers should insist on decent, responsible behavior from their students. Teacher failure is synonymous with failure to maintain adequate classroom discipline. Many teachers labor under false assumptions about discipline. They believe that firm control is stifling and inhumane. It is not. Firm control maintained correctly is humane and liberating.

Key Idea #2

Teachers have basic educational rights in their classrooms, including the right to establish optimal learning environments; the right to determine, request, and expect appropriate behavior from their students; and the right to receive help from administrators and parents when it is needed. Figures 3.2, 3.3, and 3.4 illustrate approaches to working with parents and logging discipline occurrences.

Key Idea #3

Students also have basic rights in the classroom, including the right to have teachers who help them limit their inappropriate, self-destructive behavior; the right to have teachers who provide positive support for their appropriate behavior; and the right to choose how to behave, with full understanding of the consequences that automatically follow their choices. Figures 3.5 and 3.6 illustrate strategies for setting expectations.

Key Idea #4

These needs, rights, and conditions are best met through assertive discipline, in which the teacher clearly communicates expectations to students and consistently follows up with appropriate actions but never violates the best interests of the students. This assertive discipline consists of the following elements: identifying expectations clearly; willingness to say "I like that" and "I don't like that"; persistence in stating expectations and feelings; use of firm tone of voice; maintenance of eye contact; and use of nonverbal gestures in support of verbal statements.

Assertive discipline enables teachers to do such things as say no, without feeling guilty; give and receive compliments genuinely and gracefully; express thoughts and feelings that others might find intimidating; stand up for feelings and rights when under fire from others; comfortably place demands on others; firmly influence students' behavior without yelling and threatening; and work more successfully with chronic behavior problems.

Teachers who use assertive discipline do the following: employ assertive response styles, as distinct from nonassertive or hostile response styles; eliminate negative expectations about student behavior; establish and communicate clear expectations for positive

Dear Parent: In order to guarantee your child, and all the students in my classroom, the excellent learning climate they deserve, I am utilizing the following Discipline Plan starting today.

My philosophy: I believe all my students can behave appropriately in my classroom. I will tolerate no student stopping me from teaching and/or any student from learning.

My Class Rules

1. _____
2. _____
3. _____
4. _____
5. _____

If a Student Chooses to Break a Rule

1st consequence _____
2nd consequence _____
3rd consequence _____
4th consequence _____
5th consequence _____
Severe disruption _____

Students Who Behave Will Earn

_____
_____

It is in your child's best interest that we work together in relationship to his/her schooling. I will thus be in close contact with you regarding your child's progress in my classroom. Please sign the tear-off and have your child bring it with him/her to school tomorrow. If you have any questions or comments, please feel free to call me or write them on the tear-off.

Sincerely yours,

Dear

I read and understood the Discipline Plan for your classroom.

_____
Parent/Guardian Signature

Figure 3.2. Sample Discipline Plan Letter to Parents

Guidelines For Working With Parents

___ Accept you have a right to their help
___ Assert yourself immediately
___ Send home positive notes
___ Reinforce parents who support you
___ Send home copy of your Discipline Plan
___ Don't always believe what parents say
___ Call fathers
___ Call parents at work

Before Meeting or Talking With Parents Fill Out:

Goals for Conference (I need your cooperation)

_____

Objectives for Conference (I want you to . . .)

_____

_____

Rationale for Conference (It is in your child's best interest that we work together to help him/her)

_____

_____

Consequences You Feel Will Occur If The Parents Do Not Cooperate (If you do not cooperate the result will be . . .)

_____

_____

Documentation of Your Assertions

_____

Figure 3.3. Teacher/Parent Conference Worksheet

If you have severe behavior problems, keep the following record:

Student's Name	Date	Rules Broken	Consequences You Provided Negative & Positive

Figure 3.4. Discipline Record Sheet

CLASSROOM BEHAVIOR RULES
Students Will:
1.
2.
3.
4.

Figure 3.5. Classroom Behavior Rules

student behavior; use hints, questions, and I-messages rather than demands for requesting student behavior; use eye contact, gestures, and touches to supplement verbal messages; follow through with promises rather than with threats; and be assertive in confrontations with students, including statements of expectations, consequences that will occur, and why the action is necessary.

To become more assertive in discipline, teachers should do the following things: practice assertive response styles; set clear limits and consequences; follow through consistently; make specific assertive discipline plans and rehearse them mentally; write things down—do not trust the memory; practice the broken-record technique for repeating expectations; and ask school principals and parents for support in the efforts to help students.

DISCIPLINE PLAN

If You Break A Rule

1st Time	
2nd Time	
3rd Time	
4th Time	
5th Time	
Severe Disruption	

Figure 3.6. Discipline Plan

When Something Extra Is Required

Problem-Solving Teams

As outlined in Chapter 3, classroom teachers have available to them several procedures to maintain an orderly and well-managed classroom. Circumstances arise occasionally, though, that demand resources, skills, or perspectives that may not be accessible in the classroom. Some students exhibit extreme behaviors that are resistant to modification within the classroom. Others experience stressors within their homes or communities that may cause inappropriate classroom behaviors, and still others display undesirable behaviors as a result of academic or curricular difficulties. Sometimes the intensity or pervasiveness of these difficulties extends the teacher's skills and resources to the point that additional support may be needed. When such problems occur, it is important for the school to have a formal procedure to provide assistance upon the teacher's request.

We have found that an attractive mechanism for providing this assistance is the school-based problem-solving team. Problem-solving teams consist of groups of educational personnel, parents, and other involved parties that meet systematically to discuss problems referred to them by other educational personnel within their school. Although these problems often primarily constitute educational or behavioral problems within the classroom, some teams also address specific school problems within their mission, such as at-risk students, substance abuse prevention, or dropout programs. Problem-solving teams provide a collegial source of assistance to teachers that exists outside of the classroom, yet involves minimal bureaucratic requirements such as extensive paperwork. By involving teachers and parents both as expert resources and as collaborators in problem solving, problem-solving teams also may increase commitment, communication, and morale in both groups.

School-based teams offer a number of important advantages for solving discipline problems. They provide a noninvasive decision-making mechanism for developing and coordinating interventions for identified or referred students. In addition, they maximize parent and teacher involvement in, ownership of, and responsibility for classroom discipline. Problem-solving teams that emphasize imparting problem-solving knowledge and participation, that allow for multiple intervention selection opportunities, and that provide follow-up by building staff also may improve overall school-based decision making. Further, because the problem-solving team concept is a building-based problem-solving model, it corresponds conceptually with the current political climate of educational reform with its emphasis on site-based management and teacher empowerment. Finally, school-based teams provide a collaborative communication mechanism for secondary schools, which may lack such structures.

School-based problem-solving teams cultivate and institutionalize problem solving in the classroom and collaboration among professionals and parents at the school level. The school-based team identifies needs, receives referrals, and plans and coordinates interventions with teachers, parents, other educational personnel, and community agencies. Under the direction of the team, preventive interventions, crisis intervention, case management, and interagency coordination may be provided by school personnel. Teams may constitute a valuable framework for providing the following: (a) help for teachers in dealing with educational, behavioral, and discipline needs of students; (b) early identification and schoolwide prevention of educational, behavioral, and discipline problems; (c) a means of in-school intervention for students with difficult discipline problems who historically have been excluded from school attendance or who drop out at the secondary level; and (d) a mechanism for referral of students with educational, behavioral, and discipline problems to appropriate educational resources.

School-based problem-solving teams have received steadily increasing attention, both as a regular education remedy for difficult educational, behavioral, and discipline problems and as an alternative to traditional test/label/place service delivery for problem children (Fuchs & Fuchs, 1990; Hayek, 1987; Kirk, 1986; National Association of School Psychologists, 1986; Ogden & Germinario, 1988; Rich & Heintzelman, 1989). Although several team models have been outlined (e.g., Chalfant, Pysh, & Moultrie, 1979; Fuchs & Fuchs, 1990; Graden, Casey, & Christenson, 1985; Ogden & Germinario, 1988), the basic goal of most team models has been to provide a mechanism for solving children's educational and behavioral problems instead of or prior to referring them for formal assessment for special educational placement (Braden, 1988). At the secondary level, problem-solving teams may focus on dropout prevention, substance abuse, school violence, and so on.

The problem-solving team model that has the longest history is the Teacher Assistance Team (TAT) model proposed by Chalfant and associates (Chalfant & Pysh, 1981; Chalfant & Pysh, 1989; Chalfant, Pysh, & Moultrie, 1979). Chalfant's model consists of a team of regular education teachers meeting on a scheduled basis to generate solutions to problem referrals from parents, students, or other teachers in the school. The number of teams in each school varies, depending on the student population and number of referrals; however, a typical TAT may meet once a week throughout the school year to handle referrals. The team refers only the most intractable problems for possible special education services or for additional community services. The TAT model is attractive because it reduces special education assessment costs, requires no additional staff, and requires minimal time commitments (Chalfant, Pysh, &

Moultrie, 1979). According to Chalfant and colleagues, one major benefit of TAT implementation is improved handling of regular classroom problems and the decrease in inappropriate referrals to special education.

Building Teams: Practical Considerations

Although problem-solving teams can make an important contribution to school and classroom discipline, instituting them calls for considerable skill, commitment, and planning. Serving on a problem-solving team often requires additional time commitments and planning responsibilities. Team membership requires a belief in the effectiveness of systematic, collaborative problem solving, along with interpersonal skills to facilitate such collaboration. Administrative backing and flexibility in accommodating team functioning are powerful elements of team influence. For these reasons, selecting, developing, and supporting team members is a crucial component of successful problem-solving teams.

1. In most cases, teams should be composed of volunteers. Peer and self-nominations often are effective ways to develop a pool of potential team members, but final selection should be determined by willingness and commitment to participate diligently in team process. Our experience in consulting with numerous schools is that a core of these dedicated educators is available in almost every school.

2. School administrators should provide resources and support whenever possible to facilitate team functioning. These might include a stable meeting place, some additional free time for meetings, and recognition for serving on the team. In addition, the principal's participation often is crucial to team influence.

3. School teams seldom are able to function effectively without some training in team development and process. As discussed earlier, teachers may have divergent beliefs about the way children learn and should behave. Some mechanisms for dealing with these differences are an important

part of the team-building process. Typically, groups require a period of acquaintance and trust building prior to being able to work as a unit to solve problems. Also, training in collaboration, interventions, and consultation may be necessary to teach interventions and problem-solving skills to educational personnel who are not members of the team. Finally, ongoing monitoring of and consultation on team functioning may help to solve conflicts and other group problems that sometimes arise as groups develop. Such consultation usually is available within the school system from school psychologists, who often have been trained in group process. An additional benefit of involvement of support personnel such as school psychologists is their knowledge of learning and behavioral interventions.

4. Teams should be enabled to make use of their collective expertise. Team decisions need teacher and administrative support, along with open communication channels with administrators and support personnel, to be effective in solving discipline problems. Ideally, problem-solving teams should serve as school-based resources for teachers, parents, administrators, support personnel, and community services. This relationship is portrayed in Figure 4.1.

5. In addition to the collective expertise of the problem-solving team, each team member brings to the team a unique perspective based on knowledge and experience and a set of beliefs about learning, teaching, and behavior. Recognition of and respect for the contribution of each team member encourages the expression of that member's expertise in group problem solving, resulting in better solutions. Promoting each member's participation requires considerable skill and sensitivity, but should increase the quality of the team's solutions as well as the influence it has in implementing them.

Team Configuration

An important component of problem-solving team success is its composition. Whereas membership requirements should be

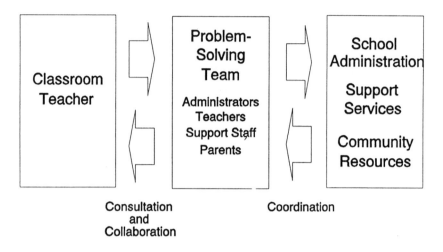

Figure 4.1. School-Team-Community Communication

flexible and may vary from school to school, diverse representation increases the breadth of expertise and influence on the team. Perhaps the most critical team members are teachers. Teacher participation is important to foster commitment and to provide current and ongoing expertise in classroom management. In addition, teacher membership and leadership increase the face validity of the procedure with other teachers in the school while taking advantage of teacher communication networks. Representation on the team by other school professionals, parents, and occasional community representatives further improves the breadth and depth of team strategies. The membership of a typical problem-solving team might include the following:

Teachers. Teacher membership should emphasize regular education teachers. Although special educators can bring significant expertise to classroom management, it is important to remember that regular education classrooms vastly outnumber special education classrooms, and that regular educators have the most knowledge about what occurs in classrooms in their school. Also, a basic premise of school-based problem-solving teams is that teachers possess sufficient means to discover effective strategies for solving their problems provided they are given the needed opportunity and resources. Between two and four teachers should be permanent members of the problem-solving team; optimally, one of these should serve as chair of the team.

School administrators. Administrators bring valuable managerial expertise and position power to the team, further enhancing both the quality and impact of team strategies. Also, they contribute an understanding of school- and system-level policy and a communication link with upper administrators. However, school administrators as team members sometimes must monitor their involvement in team meetings because other team members may tend to respond to their position rather than their expertise. That is, other team members may either defer to or challenge administrator perspectives because of his or her administrative status. In some instances, this behavior may increase the efficiency of team decisions, but in most cases it also will decrease commitment to resulting decisions. Typically, an administrator is included as a permanent team member.

School-based support personnel. Additional special skills may be necessary for quality team decisions. Although these skills may vary from case to case, continuing contributions in behavior management and discipline, along with perspectives on team process and functioning, are fundamental needs of most problem-solving teams. For this reason, problem-solving teams often include members other than teachers and administrators. As previously mentioned, school psychologists have training in behavior management and group process that makes them valuable additions to problem-solving teams. Other support personnel who may contribute such expertise are school counselors and special education teachers. However, support team members should serve as resources rather than as team leaders; their knowledge bases are necessary, but ancillary, components of the team. Typically, no more than one school-based support person should serve as a permanent team member. Additional support personnel should be available as resources on team request.

Other school personnel. Temporary team members often are included in team meetings depending on the nature of the problem and team needs. These may include teachers, support personnel, janitorial or cafeteria staff, administrators or supervisors, secretaries, and other personnel as they are available and needed. Perhaps most important, school personnel who initially seek help in solving an educational, behavioral, or discipline problem should be included as a functioning team member until the presented problem is solved in a satisfactory manner. This involvement serves two purposes. First, it provides the referring teacher with strategies and support for solving the problem at hand. Second, it models a collaborative problem-solving strategy for the referring teacher, giving the teacher a general strategy for solving subsequent similar problems. In this way, a network of collegial problem solving gradually develops within the school.

Parents. Parents are a critical and often neglected source of expertise for team problem solving. Ironically, they often are relegated to minor, temporary roles in serving the educational needs of their children. Although many parents are comfortable with this relationship, a number of them have the willingness and the skill to contribute significantly to the education and discipline of their children. A fundamental facet of parent/team collaboration is a mutual, positive respect for the perspective and knowledge that each brings to the education of the student. Because discipline often involves negative interactions among teachers, students, and parents, blame sometimes becomes easier than cooperation. Negotiating with parents as colleagues and integral members of the problem-solving team requires great skill, particularly during crises. However, solving initial problems and preventing subsequent difficulties demand such efforts.

Through both our research and our experience, we have become increasingly aware of the important role that parents play in the development and education of their children. We also are aware of wariness with which many school personnel approach parents and the alienation from schools that many parents feel. This adversarial relationship is unfortunate because of the necessary and virtual dependence that schools and parents have in educating children.

Particularly in working with difficult-to-teach children, effective discipline may be almost impossible without the active participation of parents as equal partners with the school.

Team Training

Determining the membership of the school problem-solving team represents only the first step in building effective decision-making units. Considerable additional preparation of the school and the team needs to occur to ensure that necessary skills, knowledge, process, and perspectives are available for effective school discipline. Although resources for such preparation often may be available within the school system for relatively minimal initial start-up cost, their importance should not be overlooked. Preparation for implementation of problem-solving teams should occur on at least three levels: the school system, the school, and the school team. For maximum effectiveness, preparation at these levels should be coordinated and sequenced carefully.

At the first level, system-level administrators and supervisors should be apprised of the nature and purpose of school-based problem-solving teams. Because administrative support is crucial to the success of school-based interventions, initial presentation and approval of problem-solving teams should be followed up with consistent, systematic communication about the progress of implementation and any outcomes that accrue.

At a second level, the school in which the problem-solving team will function should be prepared for the initiation of the system. Because teacher input and participation are particularly important to the success of problem-solving teams, this preparation probably should start before approaching system-level administration; that is, classroom teachers should be involved in every step of the planning and proposal process. This involvement increases commitment to and subsequent implementation of the team process while assuring that the mechanism will be acceptable to the school. As part of the preparation process, training of teachers and educational staff within the school about problem-solving teams and their relationship to them should occur. However, it is important to note that this training must not take the place of integral teacher involvement in the planning and implementation process.

Also, final implementation should take into account teacher feedback in such a way that the problem-solving team is tailored to the characteristics of the school in which it functions. To inform teachers about problem-solving teams to aid them in this feedback, the following training dimensions should be presented and discussed: (a) the team model and the purpose of school-based problem-solving teams; (b) types of discipline, educational, and behavioral concerns that are appropriate for referral to the problem-solving team; (c) the referral and the referral process; (d) the composition of the team and how it was/will be determined; (e) outcomes that can be expected from team problem solving; and (f) expectations for teacher contribution to and participation in the team.

The third level of preparation involves training of the team itself. The team is not required to have expertise in all problems that might be referred to it, but should have strategies and resources for securing such expertise as needed. Also, it is expected that team members bring considerable expertise for solving classroom problems to the team, and that an important training need is a mechanism for coordinating and implementing this expertise. Therefore, team training should constitute a combination of content knowledge and skills along with process expertise in team functioning and group decision making. Some areas of team training are (a) group process and group decision making, (b) consultation and collegial collaboration, (c) stages of problem solving, (d) interprofessional and interagency coordination, (e) school-based service alternatives, (f) special education rules and eligibility requirements, (g) classroom and organizational discipline models and strategies, and (h) school system policies and regulations.

Referrals

One of the first decisions that the newly constituted team must make is how to solicit and process requests for assistance. Limitations on teacher time and resources may discourage completion of long or complicated referral forms; however, it is important for the team to have sufficient information about the situation to make

TABLE 4.1 Sample Questions for Request for Assistance

Name of child

Age

Birth date

Grade

Name of referring teacher

Description of desired behavior

Description of current behavior (both strengths and problems)

Strategies already used by referring teacher

Background information

initial judgments about how to handle the referral. Some compromise between referral requirements and needed information may be necessary to encourage teacher participation in the problem-solving process. Whenever additional information is needed, interview and observation contacts can be negotiated, allowing the team to minimize the paperwork needed for the initial request for assistance. Also, the use of checklists and surveys can facilitate and structure the referral process for the teacher. Although individual request for assistance forms should be developed to be appropriate for the individual school, some general questions that we have encountered and that probably will appear on most forms are presented in Table 4.1.

Team Problem Solving

Problem-solving teams often can generate efficient and effective problem solutions by using a general problem-solving model

TABLE 4.2 Steps in Team Problem Solving

Define the problem

Specify the problem

Identify possible solutions

Select solution(s)

Negotiate implementation of solution(s)

Implement solution(s)

Evaluate solution(s)

Follow up and recycle if necessary

---

to process discipline referrals. Although writers have differed on the number of steps in their problem-solving sequences, we have found general agreement on broad stages and their sequence. These stages provide a useful general heuristic framework for solving school problems. At every stage, the referring teacher is integrally involved with team members in determining the nature and extent of the problem and its solution. A fundamental assumption of this procedure is that the problem is the responsibility of the referring teacher, whereas the team's responsibility is to provide a problem-solving framework, to contribute expertise, and to coordinate resources for solving the problem. General problem-solving steps are presented in Table 4.2.

Define the problem. Problem definition is a negotiated process on which subsequent steps pivot. Therefore, its importance to the problem-solving process may outstrip other team activities. Problem definition begins with the referral statement, but typically involves clarification to arrive at a workable problem statement. For example, a referral problem that states "he spends most of his class time daydreaming" is quite descriptive but may have different meanings depending on one's perspective. Additional clarification of "most of his class time" and "daydreaming" probably are necessary to get a grasp on the problem meaning intended by the referring teacher. For example, does "most of his class time" mean instructional time or independent work time? Morning or afternoon? Every day or Monday or Friday? Does "daydreaming" mean staring out the window or doodling? Failing to do written work or failing to participate in discussion? Answers to these and other questions help to clarify the exact nature and extent of the problem. Much of the time, problem definition involves reducing the presenting problem to observable terms on which the teacher and the team can agree.

Specify the problem. Additional understanding of the nature of the problem is necessary before relevant problem solutions can be generated. This understanding includes the settings in which the discipline problem occurs and does not occur, consequences and payoffs for the behavior, and previous strategies attempted by the teacher to solve the problem. In this way, the function of the behavior in the classroom can be ascertained and interventions to alter the behavior often become apparent. It is at this stage that awareness of the need for additional support from outside the classroom sometimes becomes evident.

Identify possible solutions. Appropriate interventions for problem solution often will arise from the collective expertise of the team via team discussions of the problem. However, the absence of an apparent solution may necessitate the use of brainstorming possible resolutions, or seeking additional information or expertise for redefining the problem. Brainstorming has been proposed for many years as an effective tool for generating creative solutions in groups. It involves an open, noncritical forum for solution generation that discourages evaluation or selection until a number of inventive possibilities are produced. Often, initially extreme suggestions become more promising upon subsequent examination and may yield ingenious alternatives to apparently intractable problems.

Select solution(s). Strategy selection should occur only after a list of possible alternatives has been developed. Identification of specific criteria for evaluating solutions may be helpful in this process and should be negotiated and agreed on in each case. Some general criteria include the amount of time required for potential solutions, their relative intrusiveness in the classroom and the school, additional resources and expertise they may require, their complexity, their legality, and so on. Whatever the criteria decided upon by the term, they should be applied to alternatives systematically with the goal of arriving at the most promising one or two solutions. Of course, agreement by the referring teacher on the desirability of potential solutions should be an important ingredient in strategy selection.

Negotiate implementation of solution(s). How solutions that have been selected should be implemented requires the team's careful consideration. Some solutions require additional time, resources, or staffing for successful implementation. Because these areas often are in short supply in public schools, administrators, the team, and referring teachers may need to consider possible alternatives. However, in every case it is important to involve the referring teacher in negotiations, and the referring teacher should assume responsibility for implementing interventions whenever possible. Even when additional temporary support is necessary, the referring teacher can learn new skills and perspectives in approaching similar problems by assuming responsibility for disposing of the current problem.

Implement solution(s). Strategy implementation should be planned carefully with as much team support as necessary. Optimally, the referring teacher will be able to implement solutions within the classroom to solve the problem. Implementation of additional solutions may require school resources, alternative placements, system-level support, parent involvement, or even community backing.

Evaluate solution(s). Determining the effectiveness of problem solution strategies aids in evaluating interventions as well as the usefulness of the team itself. This information should guide subsequent efforts and provide feedback through which team functioning can be adjusted. Procedures for program evaluation should be a formal component of the problem solution plan developed by the team in negotiation with the referring teacher. As much as possible, evaluation strategies should be minimally intrusive and should require as few additional resources from the solution implementers as is feasible.

Follow up and recycle if necessary. Depending on the results of evaluation of solution implementation, it may be necessary to reformulate the problem or to devise additional strategies to solve the problem. Regardless of the results of evaluation, the team should follow up the problem-solving interaction with the referring teacher to determine long-term results and teacher satisfaction with the problem-solving team.

Conclusions: Evidence From Research

Although school-based problem-solving teams are a promising tool for dealing with educational and behavioral problems, the effectiveness of school-based problem-solving teams has received mixed research support (Lloyd, Crowley, Kohler, & Strain, 1988). Chalfant and Pysh (1989) noted in their survey that schools using TATs reported lowered referral rates to special education, high rates of teacher satisfaction, and high reported rates of problem resolution. Graden, Casey, and Bonstrom (1985) found that four of the six public schools in their study reduced special education referrals following implementation of prereferral teams. On the other hand, Harrington and Gibson (1986) reported that only 50% of the teachers in their study rated prereferral teams as being helpful with problem referrals. Also, Braden (1988) reported lack of clarity of goals and disagreement about usefulness in his study of teachers' perceptions of prereferral teams.

One explanation for these findings may be variability in building-level support for this intervention. As has been asserted throughout this book, an organizational discipline perspective may be necessary to implement effective problem-solving teams. Consistent, planned support and resources from school system administration are critical in maintaining optimal effectiveness of school-based teams (Short & Talley, 1990). General training in participative decision making, administrative support and funding, and sensitization to the needs of children may be responsible for changes in the ways that schools deal with children with behavior problems. Problem-solving teams constitute only one facet of programmatic emphasis, politics, training, and support that occur within the social system of the school. As noted by Ponti, Zins, and Graden (1988), whether and how discipline strategies are implemented may depend on organizational and system variables.

Special Concerns

Discipline and Strategies for Students At-Risk

S tudents who exhibit recurrent discipline problems in school often display other characteristics that distinguish them from their classmates. In addition to differing from discipline norms, they may be low achievers and show little interest in school activities. In fact, these aspects occur together so frequently that they may offer a reasonable description of a current and familiar educational concern: the at-risk student. Because at-risk students constitute a complex and difficult educational problem, school discipline in relation to this group may raise special concerns. In this chapter, we discuss some of these issues and present some recommendations for resolving them. Much of the work behind these recommendations derives from results from a grant-funded project directed by the second author, R. J. Short (Short, Meadows, & Moracco, 1992).

A number of programs and strategies have been implemented to serve children who are at risk of school failure, and some of these have been reported in the literature. Leatt (1987) found that in-school suspension programs may be a useful strategy for dealing with disruptive at-risk students, provided they are implemented on a supportive foundation and include broad-based planning and participation. Rubel reviewed the literature on police/school collaboration in dealing with law-breaking at-risk students. He noted wide divergence in the type of programs implemented and in their effectiveness (Rubel, 1986). Yanossy reported on the effects of a multidimensional program for 20 at-risk students with chronic discipline problems, finding that program interventions were related to more positive attitudes toward school and decreased referrals to the alternative school. However, reductions in discipline problems were quite small (Yanossy, 1986).

Many discipline programs for at-risk students have focused on changing students identified as potential failures. However, such interventions may neglect the complex, systemic nature of the problem, and therefore may misidentify the problem. As noted in Chapter 1, identifying and intervening with at-risk students actually may increase their alienation to school with only minimal impact on discipline problems. In addition, services for these youth often have been limited by numerous constraints, including both lack of resources and mechanisms and lack of coordination of available resources. By reformulating the problem of discipline with respect to at-risk students in systemic, developmental terms, schools can use existing resources to develop effective discipline strategies while maintaining commitment to school in at-risk youth (Chalker, 1990; Short, Meadows, & Moracco, 1992). However, several factors should be considered in developing discipline programs for at-risk children in the public schools (Frymier, 1989). These include: (a) the systemic nature of risk for school failure; (b) difficulties in defining and identifying at-risk youth; (c) problems of using traditional discipline strategies with at-risk children; and (d) lack of coordination and communication with other agencies in solving the complex problems.

The Systemic Nature of Risk

Children and youth considered to be at-risk are those who likely will fail academically and socially without supplementary

TABLE 5.1 Characteristics of an At-Risk Child

1. Has not been advanced to next grade because of poor academics.
2. Has not mastered the basic expected skills in the curriculum.
3. Is below grade level in academic skills based on test scores.
4. Has an irregular or poor attendance record.
5. Has a record of in-school or out-of-school suspensions.
6. Is achieving significantly below ability.
7. Qualifies for free or reduced-price lunch.
8. Has a history of high mobility, either within or between districts.
9. Has experienced child abuse or neglect.
10. Is a substance abuser.
11. Has experienced racial, cultural, or gender bias.
12. Is a teen parent.
13. Has been reared in a dysfunctional home.
14. Has suffered long-term health problems.
15. Doesn't participate in school activities.

support and interventions. Most are subject to environmental, familial, or societal forces over which they often have little control and that hinder their ability to learn in school and survive in society (McCormick, 1989). A large proportion of school-age children either are or will be poor, multicultural/minority, and from nontraditional homes—all characteristics that have been related to school and social failure. As can be seen in Table 5.1, many of these and other important risk factors, which may have a profound effect on development and performance, are largely extrinsic to the child.

Examination of these characteristics reinforces the idea that children are not isolated entities; rather, they develop within and are molded by an ecological context. At-risk status results from an interaction of environmental stressors and individual characteristics. Thus, addressing environmental factors in the school and community may be at least as important and effective as firm rules and consequences in solving school discipline problems with at-risk students. Although discipline strategies for at-risk youth should not be ignored, additional intervention foci may be necessary to effect meaningful change.

Difficulties in Identifying and Defining At-Risk Students

An issue that is related to the nature of risk is the way that at-risk is defined by policymakers and practitioners. Several important concerns have arisen from various attempts at defining at-risk (Hrncir & Eisenhart, 1991). Because these points have an impact on discipline for at-risk students, they should receive careful consideration in developing such services.

First, *at-risk* is a nebulous term that often does not delineate clearly the group that it is used to describe. As can be seen from the characteristics previously discussed, risk factors include a range of social, cultural, environmental, economic, and personal components. Because some of these factors often are emphasized over others, different children may be considered to be at-risk in different settings or even at different times within the same setting. Also, even students who have endured significant stressors often manage to succeed academically and socially—sometimes to the surprise of caregivers! Therefore, care must be taken to avoid facile use of the term to describe any child or group of children. Such lack of clarity may result in miscommunication among service providers or misidentification of students.

Second, many risk factors are not static, and at-risk identification is not immutable. Students sometimes confront circumstances that may increase the risk of their experiencing academic and socioemotional difficulties (e.g., divorce, death, family crisis, working too many hours, becoming ill). Even students who have encountered few of these risk factors in their history may respond negatively to acute stressors, increasing the chances of discipline problems and academic and social failure. Conversely, circumstances may occur to stabilize the environment so that the student's ability to succeed is enhanced, even in a context of profoundly negative environmental and personal characteristics. Again, careful evaluation of status and progress within a systemic frame is important in developing and implementing effective discipline interventions for these students.

Third, identification of at-risk youth using superficial assessment of indicators of risk, including test scores, often provides inadequate estimates of their characteristics. Defining at-risk in terms of test scores, surveys, and so forth also may result in simplistic and/or inaccurate formulations of the nature and constitution of target groups. At worst, casual labeling of students as being at-risk based on oversimplified, unproven, or unsound procedures may exacerbate risk factors by increasing alienation in identified youth (Caterall, 1987). A related issue is the use of at-risk identification procedures without the availability of specific, appropriate interventions to remediate at-risk status. Such lack of interventions may result in attaching an at-risk designation to a group of students without concomitant programming to alleviate concerns. Again, several intrinsic effects of labeling may occur, including isolation, reduction in involvement, and lowered expectations.

Limitations of Traditional Discipline Strategies for At-Risk Students

Discipline strategies for at-risk students often include developing pull-out programming to be implemented during the school day. These pull-out programs traditionally require identification of these children and absence from regular classes. Although these strategies are widespread and are relatively easy to implement, they have been criticized for several reasons (Caterall, 1987). Pull-out programs may require a high level of commitment and additional effort by school personnel. Many times, these programs depend on classroom teachers for initial identification of at-risk students. Requiring additional paperwork to accomplish this identification often places another burden on teachers' full schedules. Some do not consider this as part of their expected job responsibilities.

Another barrier to many such programs is the difficulty of pulling out students during the typical academic day. Students who are pulled out of academic classes face the problem of having fewer class sessions to maintain academic progress within the regular classroom. These students many times are behind in class already. Because of the difficulties inherent in planning activities before or after school, there is not enough time in most school days to provide for additional services ,without creating additional problems for the students. Also, many school systems mandate a set number of minutes of classroom instruction that may be impossible to meet if students are removed from classrooms.

Pull-out programs that call for additional services for students also require personnel to provide these services. Although this can be handled by hiring additional staff, many school budgets cannot support such added expenses. Another alternative is to allow volunteers, either professional or paraprofessional, to come into the school setting and provide services. However, volunteers may not have the necessary qualifications, or their agenda may not be consonant with the school's mission.

Lack of Coordination of Services
With Other Groups

One potentially powerful prevention strategy is coordinating family and community resources to deter discipline problems in these multiproblemed youth. However, service coordination has been identified as the single greatest deficiency in service delivery to children (Knitzer, 1984). Although coordination of available services in rural areas and areas with few resources may be critical in serving the needs of at-risk children, service roles and responsibilities often are limited to a single model and/or setting. In schools, for example, teachers are acknowledged to be the primary, and often the only, service providers for children. For most exceptional children, services are coordinated within the school or school system by multidisciplinary teams via the individualized education program. Systematic planning and coordination of services beyond the school's purview may be relatively uncommon.

However, at-risk children often have multiple problems, requiring them to be served by several agencies in addition to and/or outside the schools. Because no formal provisions exist for case coordination and collaboration between agencies, these children frequently move back and forth among agencies with no agency or profession accepting responsibility for treatment (Friedman, 1986; Friedman & Stroul, 1988). Also, different agencies and professions often are unaware of different policies and legislation that regulate services provided by other agencies and professions. As a result, problem children often participate in a cycle of uncoordinated assessment and referral from agency to agency that yields frustration to parents and lack of services to their children (Knitzer, 1984; Saxe, Cross, & Silverman, 1988). Such coordination, particularly across agencies, continues to be a significant bottleneck in service provision to children (Mearig, 1982). In writing about children's mental health policy, Saxe, Cross, and Silverman (1988) note that cross-agency coordination of children's mental health services is almost nonexistent. Combined with practical problems noted above, these conceptual problems constitute a significant concern in providing services to at-risk students.

School/Community Programs
for At-Risk Youth: An Example

In our project to serve at-risk youth, we found that effective discipline for at-risk youth requires an emphasis on developing an organized, school-based problem-solving program to identify and coordinate services for at-risk children with discipline problems. In addition, programs need to emphasize collaboration with other agencies to establish a coordinated service delivery network. The combination of these two activities allows schools to prevent chronic discipline problems in this population by dealing with some of the causes of these behaviors. They also provide an avenue for providing assistance to teachers on the occurrence of such behaviors.

Our project worked to develop an integrated combination of four components. The first component, also described in more detail in Chapter 4, is the school-based problem-solving team. To deal with difficult discipline problems, each school should develop a school-based team consisting of an administrator, volunteer teachers, and other members as needed. Whenever appropriate and practical, the team also included community agency representatives. In fact, several of our teams also included a local minister as a member, and one of our teams included the superintendent's wife. The school-based team identifies needs, receives referrals, plans interventions, and coordinates services.

A second component in successful programs for at-risk children is referral, or identification strategies. Because risk factors in school failure have been identified in recent legislation and literature to be multidimensional, the method of identification should reflect the multiple determinants of risk, while minimizing the effect of labeling. This procedure includes review of cumulative records, teacher nomination forms, and self-report measures. Schools should implement a broad-based prevention program that identifies factors that contribute to discipline problems and develops ways to moderate them. Because each school is unique, schools should tailor programs to their individual needs rather than simply adopting one of the myriad packaged programs that are now becoming available. In addition, school-based teams should work to sensitize their schools to psychometric and labeling issues in the identification procedure. In this way, each school's sophistication in recognizing at-risk factors and in judging methods of gathering data will be enhanced.

Third, each school should initiate a network of school and community resources to prevent chronic or severe discipline problems. Team members may need to contact community agencies to ascertain target groups and types of services available in each agency, along with the extent to which these agencies are willing to collaborate with public schools. Catalogs of this information may be useful in preventing these serious behaviors.

Fourth, each school-based team should develop or solicit expertise in generating interventions to serve at-risk children within its school. School-based teams should be encouraged to assume leadership in developing and implementing strategies. Interventions should be developmental and instructional in nature and designed to help target children develop academic and social coping skills. As much as possible, at-risk children should continue to be educated within a systematic, planned discipline continuum rather than being excluded from school experiences.

Outcome data from projects directed by one of us have shown that school-based teams, community liaisons, and systematic identification of at-risk children are viable service delivery strategies. School-based teams in project schools collaborated with community and university resources to plan interventions for targeted youth. Community agencies consistently showed considerable interest in communicating with project schools in response to contacts with project personnel. Altogether, coordinated, comprehensive prevention services may prove most effective in dealing with difficult discipline problems.

6

What About Corporal Punishment?

The United States is one of the few developed nations in the world that continues to condone corporal punishment. Over 30 states either authorize the practice of corporal punishment or have taken no stand concerning its use. Only 16 states have legislation against the practice of corporal punishment. Corporal punishment seems to be an accepted educational practice in the United States.

Despite American failure to proscribe corporal punishment, the practice continues to be questioned by researchers and professionals. A complex and emotional issue, corporal punishment also arouses disagreement and debate among educators and the public. Proponents support their position with long tradition, biblical teachings, and claimed effectiveness. Opponents base their arguments on behavioral principles, empirical findings, and moral reasoning. In the face of these stands, the actual uses and misuses of corporal punishment are often obscured by emotion and tradition.

Corporal Punishment—Benefits and Costs

Corporal punishment conceivably might be considered to have several benefits. It may indeed suppress—but not eliminate—the behaviors in response to which it is used. It is quickly administered and apparently works quickly, particularly when used in anger. It requires no training or skill—only superior physical size and strength. It provides an outlet and a target for the punisher's anger and frustration. In considering this list, we were surprised to note an interesting point: Almost all of the benefits of corporal punishment accrue to the punisher! Relatively few positive effects for the punished child can be identified.

The costs for the use of corporal punishment, on the other hand, are ominously heavy and much more evenly shared. They include costs to the punisher, to the child, to the school, and to society. The punisher, in modeling aggression as a method of solving problems, risks retaliatory aggression from the punished child. This fact may explain the relative infrequency of the use of corporal punishment in response to adolescent misbehavior in comparison with its use with younger children. Also, the punisher may have increased difficulty in establishing open, trust-based communication with a child following the use of corporal punishment. Corporal punishment may therefore make the disciplinary efforts of the punisher more difficult and less effective than other, more positive, techniques.

Corporal punishment is also costly to children who are punished. Corporal punishment increases alienation and anxiety in children and decreases interest in and commitment to the school (Wayson, 1985). Such punishment has a similar effect on other students who have not been so punished, but who are aware of the punishment. Also, whereas corporal punishment cannot teach a child to behave appropriately in the classroom, it can teach the child avoidance and deviousness. A student can make the connection between spanking and getting caught just as easily as that student can make the connection between spanking and misbehaving. Corporal punishment thus has negative affective and behavioral effects on the punished child. At the least, these effects may make the task of learning self-discipline even harder for punished children.

Within the school, the use of corporal punishment may produce an anxious, fearful, angry, and aggressive climate. Such a climate may actually cause many of the problems that corporal punishment was originally used to remediate (Wu, Pink, Crain, & Moles, 1982). Corporal punishment may create a cycle of negative emotions and behavior that requires sterner and sterner measures to stem. Few teachers or students like to work in such a punitive, jail-like environment. Absenteeism and dropouts may often result from the negative climate caused by the use of corporal punishment.

Because corporal punishment models and legitimizes aggression, causes anxiety and withdrawal, and contributes to dropping out, it may also constitute a substantial cost to society (Bauer, Dubanoski, Yamauchi, & Honbo, 1990; Wayson, 1985). Problem solving via violence and aggression, learned in childhood, likely carries over into adulthood. Child abuse and violent crime may therefore trace their origin to corporal punishment. Adolescents who drop out to avoid corporal punishment pose an additional burden on society in their greater rates of unemployment, illiteracy, and maladaptiveness.

Alternatives to Corporal Punishment

Instead of focusing on the negative aspects of corporal punishment, we have found it helpful to think of several positive alternatives to the practice. Alternatives to corporal punishment can be organized into four levels of interventions that address individual student problems, classroomwide problems, school-level and/or support-system problems, and district- or system-level problems. This intervention scheme focuses on the most specific to the broadest level of problem resolution.

Individual Students

A number of individual interventions for behavior management or discipline problems, many with demonstrated effectiveness, are available to school personnel. Most of these also are quite efficient and require little additional training. Of these, perhaps the behavioral or behavior management techniques have the greatest demonstrated effectiveness in the research literature. Many of these involve reinforcement; some use rewards, whereas others use the removal of rewards. All of the techniques in this paradigm have two things in common: They are effective, and they do not use painful or aversive procedures; that is, punishment is not involved.

With younger children, reward approaches often are most effective. These approaches may involve, for example, attending to and reinforcing positive behaviors or reinforcing behaviors that are incompatible with targeted problem behaviors. It is important here to determine what is maintaining the problem behavior so that strategically applied rewards can have a positive effect. For example, if contingencies controlling a target behavior are not under the teacher's control (e.g., the misbehaving student is performing for the class, not for the teacher), then removal from those reinforcing contingencies may be more effective than removal of teacher reinforcement or reinforcement of incompatible behaviors. Significantly, ignoring the misbehavior in this study probably will not have an ameliorative effect.

Older students, due to their increased size, more developed behavioral repertoires, and increased autonomy, may be less responsive to interventions that directly manipulate reinforcement contingencies. Therefore, it may be harder to control these contingencies with adolescents than with elementary children. Two strategies, however, have been demonstrated to be effective in managing adolescent behavior. Both include involving adolescents and/or their parents in taking responsibility for behavior and its consequences. The first technique, contracting with problem adolescents for improved behavior, allows them to have input into defining their own problem behaviors, specifying behavioral goals toward appropriate behavior, and establishing reinforcement contingencies. Contracting also involves these adolescents in monitoring and controlling their own behavior.

The second technique, sending behavioral report cards to parents (also called home-based reinforcement), has been shown to improve negative behavior significantly in adolescents (Atkeson & Forehand, 1979). We have found this technique to be particularly useful with unmotivated students. Behavioral report cards are similar to academic report cards, but emphasize behavior—both positive and negative. Because parents often have control of contingencies not available to educational personnel, this intervention potentially is more powerful and meaningful in changing adolescents' behavior. In addition, parents benefit from increased contact with and information from the school. Home-based reinforcement requires minimal time and maintenance when compared to its potential benefits.

Another intervention, in-school suspension, has been presented earlier in this book. In-school suspension can be combined with behavioral contracting (Figure 6.1) and behavioral report cards (Figure 6.2) to produce an effective deterrent to student misbehavior. When done properly, in-school suspension may provide alternative in-school options for even very difficult-to-manage students. Significantly, in-school suspension programs may be most effective when they avoid punishment (Short & Noblit, 1985).

In particularly severe cases at both the elementary and the secondary levels, additional services often are available. Guidance counselors and school psychologists have multiple skills in counseling and behavior management programs. Alternative placements, such as crisis classrooms or alternative programs, have been used and are available for inspection as model programs and effective alternatives to corporal punishment.

Classroom Alternatives

Several classroom strategies that improve behavior without punishment are readily available to teachers. Although broad characteristics of such strategies have been presented in Chapter 3, two powerful examples of these procedures follow.

1. Teachers should develop a few clear, simple classroom rules and consequences with their classes and review them periodically to reinforce their practice and use. Whenever possible, teachers should adapt these classroom rules to changing characteristics of the class and the school year.

Behavior Contract

Date: _____

I, _____, will do the

following by _____:

    1. _____

    2. _____

    3. _____

    4. _____

When I have done the above, the following will happen:

    1. _____

    2. _____

    3. _____

    4. _____

Signed by: Witnessed by:

_____   _____

_____   _____

Figure 6.1. A Sample Behavior Contract

    2. Teachers should deliver prompt and appropriate conse-
       quences when students violate *and when they comply with*

Behavior Report Card

Date: _____

Name: _____

Marked boxes show that listed behaviors were present during the times indicated.

Behavior	Class Activity						
	1	2	3	Lunch	4	5	6
Shared with other children							
Asked for permission before leaving seat							
Completed assignments							

Observations:

Comments:

Figure 6.2. A Sample Daily Behavioral Report Card

classroom rules. For inappropriate behavior, rapid but unobtrusive interventions can stop present behavior and prevent

escalation in the future. For appropriate behavior, teachers can reinforce with free time or desirable activities. In the end, consequences should fit infractions (e.g., taking away a portion of free time or recess rather than all of that time or activity), as well as compliance.

Several other teacher behaviors may preclude the use of punishment by facilitating good classroom behavior (Kounin, 1970). One of these, which Kounin called "withitness," involves the teacher's awareness of the overall classroom process and happenings. Another, smooth and rapid transition between activities, requires the teacher's prior planning of activities and good organizational skills. A third, maintaining a positive, involved classroom climate, also influences positive student behavior, as does emphasizing on-task behaviors (Short & Short, 1988). All of these behaviors, and others, are within teachers' control and encourage good student behavior. Again, it is important to note that these are documented behavior change strategies; none involve corporal punishment and all supplant the need for its use.

Teacher Support and Training

Teachers often receive little formal training in classroom discipline in their teacher training programs. Without such training, it may be easier to resort to force and corporal punishment as a behavior control strategy. This places a burden on in-service training and workshops, which can provide an excellent way to remedy these training gaps and ineffective practices. Although they have limited effectiveness data, teacher-training programs such as Assertive Discipline (Canter, 1979) and Reality Therapy (Glasser, 1969) represent good examples of predeveloped training packages. Both of these packages are readily available and often are well accepted by teachers.

Administrative support of teachers in the area of classroom discipline and behavior management also influences student behavior (Short & Short, 1988). Principals and educational supervisors can provide individual support, information on model programs, and ongoing planning for improved discipline. They can provide opportunities for teachers and staff to share their ideas about classroom management and to support each other professionally. In difficult cases, they also effectively may intervene directly to aid the teacher.

System-Level Techniques

Several school systems have developed systemwide strategies to improve discipline without the use of corporal punishment. These techniques are proactive and preventive in nature. At a basic level, all school systems should have a written school policy or mission statement addressing the need for and steps toward positive school climate. Also, a written discipline code that describes positive expectations as opposed to punitive consequences is critical; this directly alerts students to acceptable and unacceptable behaviors in school and classroom settings. If possible, parents, school personnel, community leaders, and students all should be involved in developing the code. This involvement should increase commitment to the code and further strengthen relations with the community. Finally, a continuum of program options for extremely disruptive students should be available to teachers and administrators for special cases that necessitate a departure from the discipline code.

Clearly, many of these techniques are directed mainly toward improved classroom atmosphere and school climate. However, research has documented that increased student involvement and decreased levels of disruptive behavior are directly related to positive school environment. Because corporal punishment often engenders fear and aversion, it is difficult to maintain an affirmative milieu where the threat of corporal punishment is present. Although eliminating the use of corporal punishment may not result automatically in a positive school environment, it may set the stage for more positive interactions with students, parents, and school officials. Schools that do not use corporal punishment may be more positive environments with more involved students and teachers. As a result, such schools may actually experience fewer discipline problems than schools that use corporal punishment. Also, schools that use alternatives to corporal punishment may experience fewer dropouts and fewer incidents of vandalism (Bongiovanni, 1979).

The New Discipline in Practice

An Administrator's Perspective

When all is said and done, we know that student discipline continues to be the most consistently discussed problem in the public schools and the problem that most plagues educators. As mentioned earlier, discipline traditionally has been someone making a decision about the appropriate punishment to match the committed "crime." Almost always the focus of discipline was, and in too many cases still is, punishment.

Successful discipline is as challenging to administrators as modern medical practices are to the hocus-pocus rituals of tribal medicine men. Reale (1966) has noted, "The task of the teacher on his job is to translate the principles of democratic discipline into daily action in the classroom" (p. 254). Upon reflection, we find a question about how democratic our public schools are and can be.

The two national reports, *A Nation At Risk* and *High School: A Report on Secondary Education in America*, caused many, both inside and outside education, to reassess the problems of discipline management. The resulting educational discipline movement produced more rules and emphasized consistency in applying those rules and regulations as a desired outcome of a discipline process. Seminars, group discussions, and other forms of staff development for educators were used to achieve the consistency they sought in this movement.

However, the continuing concern among these served causes us to conclude that the current system is not working. There are continued attempts of a variety of actions along the lines of character growth or behavior adjustment. Punishment is perceived as a means and not a goal, and the mandate is to change the student's behavior while keeping the student within the educational setting (Kortz, 1986).

The response to this demand for effective discipline is more openness to local input resulting in many varied opinions and many opportunities for appeal if one party is not pleased with the result of the initial discipline outcomes. What should cause concern is that the focus is still on punishment. The absence of prevention in the discipline process is a question still to be addressed. The business of education is effective learning. An effective communication system or process is absolutely necessary for teachers to teach, for students to learn, and for individuals to be successful.

Classroom control is considered to be a prerequisite to classroom learning. The basic philosophy traditionally has been that children and youth who are well disciplined direct their interests, efforts, and abilities toward greater achievement. Those who are not disciplined waste their own individual opportunities and make learning difficult for classmates.

Eugene Manlove Rhodes, western writer, taught school in Alto, New Mexico, in 1891. His pupils remember him as an exceptional instructor. One noted, "When he called a class up to recite, he closed the textbook and stood before his class and taught. When he finished with us, there was nothing about that lesson we didn't know" (Rhodes, 1956, p. 28). But early in his teaching experience he was forced to establish himself as being in control of the classroom. The slight and scholarly Rhodes learned that some of the older male members of the one-room school planned to whip him and run him off. As he opened class one morning, Rhodes pulled his pistol from his belt, laid it on the desk, and called the class to order. Rhodes had the reputation of a man who would "fight a buzz saw with it running" (Rhodes, 1956, p. 108). This young teacher knew that classroom discipline was his job.

But what is discipline? The word and concept are derived from the Latin *discipulus* ("pupil desire to learn"). That Latin verb is different from the traditional aspect of punishment intended to correct or train that always focuses on short-term gains. Wrapped up in the Latin verb is the long-term training that is expected to produce mental as well as moral improvement.

The task is to view discipline as a system that is a part of the larger learning system. If the learning system is doing what it is supposed to do, would there be any discipline problems other than special causes? Discipline problems may result in students being uninterested, unengaged, and/or unfulfilled. Schools may need to improve the way students feel about schooling. Discipline with its present emphasis on punishment is a symptom of something amiss in the larger learning system.

The Proposal to Address the Contradiction: One School's Effort

Educators at Newman Smith High School realized that most of the students who were being seen for discipline referrals fit the profile of at-risk students. Something was needed to improve self-esteem of students. This issue had to be addressed before any significant changes in school for these youngsters would be realized. All of these students were individuals capable of doing well in school but for some reason were not performing up to their potential. These students tended to be multitime visitors in the in-house suspension program.

We struggled with strategies to improve life in school for students. All teachers were given instruction in the techniques of communication. The approach combined a series of written questions designed to guide a discussion to break the negative patterns for struggling teenagers who were searching to find their niche in a fast-changing world. It also taught people how to communicate not only with the significant others in their lives but also with people they did not know and with people they have had trouble communicating with in the past.

This process offers tools that enable the participants to get to know and understand each other. Participants look at their personal identities, their options and value systems, their emotions and how they express them, and different perspectives on effective speaking and listening. They explore how they choose their friends, how body language is read, and how to increase the possibilities of solving interpersonal problems effectively. One of the tools that guides a teenager to more mature thinking is a clear communication process. This can be taught through a questioning process that elicits understandable information from the participants. Guilford (1977) suggests that the habit of asking questions prods the brain into activity.

We found in our school that through the interactions and dialogue with students and teachers, the two prime actors in the schooling process, individuals learned to cope, successfully or unsuccessfully. Both students and teachers experienced many confrontations and possible discipline problems, in which expertise in communication skills made a major difference in how individuals felt about school and the instruction they received or gave.

The number of students who need dialogue with a teacher during the typical class period is staggering when multiplied by the number of students, hours, and classes. Yet, effective communication between the student and teacher is necessary for academic success. The ability to ask questions, respond clearly, and express ideas effectively are necessary skills for the student in the learning environment.

Hurt, Scott, and McCroskey (1978) note, "One of the clearest results from research in communication is that people are influenced primarily by those toward whom they have a positive attitude" (p. 116). In classrooms it was essential that the student, in order to accomplish the desired learning, have a positive regard for the teacher, which helped to eliminate the problems that escalate into punishment-type problems (Hurt, Scott, & McCroskey, 1978).

Final Thoughts

The image of the stern, fierce schoolmarm perseveres in the public mind; indeed, that image is cherished in many memories as a powerful force in educational backgrounds. But even if those memories are accurate, times have changed. The student population is considerably more diverse and complex now, and the problems they face are much different from those with which we dealt. This diversity requires moving beyond the timeworn punitive approaches that too often constitute discipline programs.

In many cases, these punitive approaches have interacted with complex student characteristics to produce two outcomes. First, students who experience traditional strategies become alienated from schools and education—much like their parents before them. Such alienation has been shown to lead to negative outcomes such as dropping out, substance abuse, and delinquency. Second, students who have been disciplined may become resistant and resentful in the classroom. This makes the teacher's job even more difficult. We suggest that there are ways of designing discipline approaches that build student self-discipline and self-esteem and that create an environment in schools that is receptive to the needs of all students.

Annotated Bibliography

Alpert, B. (1991). Students' resistance in the classroom. *Anthropology and Education Quarterly, 22*(4), 350-366.

Subtle forms of resistance found during ethnographic observation of two suburban high school English classes with 65 students are not found in a third class of 31 suburban high school students. The dialectical attitude of resistance and compliance is influenced by teaching approach and style of classroom interaction.

Arent, R. P. (1991). To tell the truth. *Learning, 19*(6), 72-73.

Discusses what teachers should do when older elementary students lie. Guidelines for handling the situation are presented along with suggestions for making children feel good about telling the truth. Three activities for encouraging truthfulness in the classroom are suggested.

Elliot, W. L. (1991). *RE-FOCUS Program—Redefine efforts: Focus on change under supervision* [A support program for students and teachers]. Kansas City, MO: Hickman Mills Consolidated School District 1.

The RE-FOCUS Program at Ruskin High School in Kansas City, Missouri, helps at-risk students to redefine their efforts in social behavior and academic success. When inappropriate behavior occurs and the classroom teacher needs assistance, the student is taken out of his or her regular school environment and assigned in the RE-FOCUS room. The program, an alternative to out-of-school suspension and traditional in-school suspension, keeps the student in the home school, yet not involved in the school's social environment. Seven teachers, a different one each hour, supervise the RE-FOCUS room. Each hour and day, teachers give instruction to students on their social behavior, why they were assigned, and how they can correct their behavior. The second part of the hour, the student works on academic subjects with the assistance of the supervising teacher. In addition, the student's regular teachers are encouraged to stop by the RE-FOCUS room to encourage the student. To help insure positive reinforcement for the student, negative statements are not used in the RE-FOCUS room. Academic success is promoted by teaching appropriate social skills through planned teaching, effective praise, and social skills teaching techniques. Students can be assigned to RE-FOCUS for 1 to 7 hours or for a maximum of 10 days, but are encouraged to appeal their stay after the 3-day minimum. During the program, supervising teachers, regular teachers, and administrators are responsible for documenting the students' progress. (Attachments include an hourly study schedule, a point total sheet, a daily attendance form, a social skills curriculum, a disciplinary report, and RE-FOCUS assignment sheets.)

Fernandez-Balboa, J. M. (1990). Helping novice teachers handle discipline problems. *Journal of Physical Education, Recreation and Dance, 62*(7), 50-54.

Explains factors that influence novice teachers' discipline problems to help students, novice teachers, and teacher educators deal with the problems. The article describes assertiveness as a process for dealing with and preventing such problems and discusses reasons why it can be useful and effective.

French, D. (1991). *A focus on discipline and attendance: Structuring schools for student success.* Boston: Massachusetts State Board of Education.

The effectiveness and applicability of student discipline and attendance policies in Massachusetts' public schools are addressed in this report. Following an introduction, the second section presents a review of research and examines seven assumptions about current statewide discipline and attendance practices in light of recent findings. Recommendations are made in the third section, which advocates reexamining discipline, attendance, and academic punishment policies and implementing alternatives. Suggestions are offered for school practitioners in the following areas: staff development, discipline and attendance policies, governance and structure, curriculum and instruction, classroom management, student and family support, special needs students, and assessment and planning. The fourth section presents alternative practices that have been implemented by seven Massachusetts' schools and one Connecticut school. Legal requirements for the Massachusetts' public school discipline and attendance policies are listed in the final section.

Gaustad, J. (1990). *Gangs* (Report No. 20). Eugene, OR: ERIC Clearinghouse on Educational Management, Office of Educational Research and Improvement (ED), Washington, DC. (ERIC Document Reproduction Service No. EA 52)

An increase in gang violence and mobility in the last 20 years has alarmed members of the public school community. Gang membership, formation, location, and growth are described. Strategies to counteract gang activity, such as school discipline policies, school and community prevention programs, information sharing networks, and state legislation, are discussed.

Gottfredson, D. C. (1990). *Managing adolescent behavior: A multi-year, multi-school experiment* (Report No. 50). Center for Research on Elementary and Middle Schools, Baltimore, MD: Office of Educational Research and Improvement (ED), Washington, DC.

A 3-year program was implemented in eight middle schools in the Charleston County School District (South Carolina) in fall 1986 to cope with high rates of student misconduct. The program sought to improve the clarity of school rules and the consistency of rule enforcement, classroom organization and management, frequency of communication to the home regarding student behavior, and reinforcement for appropriate behavior. The use of school improvement teams and feedback to foster program implementation is described along with numerous measures used to assess program implementation. Program results indicate that the strength and fidelity of implementation varied considerably from school to school and were tied to the level of administrator support for the program. Student conduct improved significantly in schools where the program was implemented well. Speculations about effective discipline programs conclude the document. Appended are 10 tables and 1 figure.

Hunter, D. R. (1990). *How to increase assistant principals' involvement in class management: Tips for principals from NASSP*. Reston, VA: National Association of Secondary School Principals.

Strategies for principals to increase their assistant principals' involvement in classroom management and to fulfill their positions as instructional leaders are described in this bulletin. Strategies include (a) introduction, implementation, and reinforcement of classroom management skills; (b) development of partnerships with teachers; (c) understanding and adjusting classroom dynamics; (d) establishing student responsibility; (e) use of a systematic approach to discipline; (f) involvement of all staff to create a positive atmosphere; (g) use of support services; (h) enhancement and motivation of teachers; and (i) assignment of assistant principals to different duties. The strategies stress discipline problem prevention through increased involvement in classroom management.

Layne, D. J., & Grossnickle, D. R. (1990, October 21-24). *Real school safety depends upon safe-oriented discipline policies*. Paper presented at the annual meeting of the Illinois Principals Association, Chicago, IL.

Issues relevant to the formation and implementation of clearly defined and enforceable discipline policies to maintain a secure school environment are discussed in this paper. One area of tension exists between the development of stricter discipline policies for student standards of conduct and students' constitutional rights. Conclusions are that discipline policies require school/parent cooperation, explicit standards, and cooperation between all educational stakeholders. Seven broad goals proposed by the National School Safety Center are briefly outlined. Included are examples of one school's guidelines for drug testing, identification of at-risk students, discipline policy, dress code, and athletic training rules.

Opuni, K. (1991). *Student Assignment Centers: An in-school suspension program, 1990-91.* Houston Independent School District, TX: Department of Research and Evaluation.

The effectiveness of the Student Assignment Center program (SAC), an in-school suspension program implemented in the Houston Independent School District, is evaluated in this report. The program provides instructional and counseling support services for middle school students who risk suspension or expulsion for conduct code violations. Goals are to improve students' attitudes and behaviors through motivational techniques and to improve their organizational skills and study habits. Methodology involved surveys of SAC staff, principals, and teachers at 19 participating middle schools; student attitude surveys; and analysis of program recidivism rates. Findings indicate that, overall, the program was partially effective in achieving its goals—particularly, in improving the recidivism rate and classroom environments. However, deficiencies identified by respondents formed the basis for several recommendations, one of which is to combine long- and short-term frameworks. Nine tables and six figures are included. The appendix lists SAC resources.

Roquemore, B. C. (1991, March). *The academic motivations of students who are discipline problems.* Paper presented at the annual meeting of the American Association of School Administrators, New Orleans, LA.

This study examined the academic motivation of the first students (25 from each school) in the 1990-91 school year in each of four schools in grades 9 through 12 who were suspended from school or placed in in-school suspension programs for repeated offenses (disrupting class, exhibiting aggressive behavior toward school authorities or peers, or refusing to follow directions or accept punishment). The Student Motivation Diagnostic Questionnaire was administered to the students. Findings indicated that students in all four schools scored lowest in the areas of self-concept and attitudes toward teachers. It is suggested that intervention programs could counteract students' low self-concepts and negative attitudes toward teachers. Such programs would include: parent training; teacher staff development; school programs that focus on one-on-one relationships with students; remediation of academic difficulties; and administrative monitoring of individual teachers and evaluation of the school environment. Four tables are included.

Sperry, D. J. (1990, August 12-17). *The imposition of automatic grade and credit reductions for violations of school attendance and disciplinary rules: Analysis and implications for practice.* Paper presented at the annual meeting of the National Council of Professors of Educational Administration, Los Angeles, CA.

Cases related to school policies that mandate or lead to automatic grade and/or credit reduction are reviewed in this study. Standard legal research methods were used to analyze 14 appellate and state court cases, which were categorized according to the type of sanction invoked: student suspension for violation of a disciplinary rule; automatic loss of grade points and/or credits for excessive absences; and direct treatment of unexcused absences. Findings indicate that courts are hesitant to intervene in the judgments of school officials, despite sympathy for students' rights. Recommendations for development of school discipline policies include (a) recognition of the controversial nature of such discipline policies; (b) adoption of a policy statement that clarifies the meaning of academic grades; (c) avoidance of conflict with state statutes, particularly those protecting the practice of religious beliefs; and (d) consideration of legislative enactments and/or local school board regulation as alternative measures.

Stover, D. (1992). Special discipline for special kids. *American School Board Journal, 179*(1), 40-42.

Because of the importance of preventing inappropriate disciplinary measures for special education students and those with disabilities, school boards should direct administrators to set specific procedures and limits on disciplinary measures, boost staff development programs, and establish open communication with parents.

Walker, H. M. (1990). Middle school behavioral profiles of antisocial and at-risk control boys: Descriptive and predictive outcomes. *Exceptionality: A Research Journal, 1*(1), 61-77.

In studies of school behavior adjustment involving 39 antisocial and 41 at-risk middle school boys, extremely problematic behavior profiles were found among the antisocial subjects. Profiles were quite consistent and stable across the middle school years. Predictor variables of school success or failure included math achievement, school discipline contacts, and attendance.

Webster, L., & Wood, R. W. (1990). Discipline: A problem in rural schools today? *Rural Educator, 11*(3), 19-21.

Responses of 225 South Dakota elementary school principals indicated that (a) 88% had a written discipline policy; (b) 47% followed a specific discipline model; and (c) 81% considered student discipline to be no problem or a minor problem. Responses are categorized by school district size.

References

Atkeson, B. M., & Forehand, R. (1979). Home-based reinforcement programs designed to modify classroom behavior: A review and methodological evaluation. *Psychological Bulletin, 86*(6), 1298-1308.

Bauer, G. B., Dubanoski, R., Yamauchi, L. A., & Honbo, K.A.M. (1990). Corporal punishment and the schools. *Education and Urban Society, 22*(3), 285-299.

Bloom, B. S. (1968). Learning for mastery. *Evaluation Comment, 1*(2), 5-10.

Bongiovanni, A. F. (1979). An analysis of research on punishment and its relationship to the use of corporal punishment in the schools. In I. A. Hyman & J. H. Wise (Eds.), *Corporal punishment in American education* (pp. 351-372). Philadelphia: Temple University.

Braden, J. P. (1988, August). *Do pre-referral teams work? A consumer's perspective.* Paper presented at the annual convention of the American Psychological Association, Atlanta, GA.

Brookover, W. B., & Lezotte, L. W. (1979, May). *Changes in school characteristics coincident with changes in student achievement.* Occasional Paper No. 17. East Lansing: Institute for Research on Teaching, Michigan State University.

Canter, L. (1979). Taking charge of student behavior. *National Elementary Principal, 58*(4), 33-36.

Canter, L., & Canter, M. (1981). *Assertive Discipline: Follow-up guide.* Los Angeles: Canter and Associates, Inc.

Carroll, J. B. (1963). A model of school learning. *Teachers College Record, 64,* 723-733.

Caterall, J. S. (1987). An intensive group counseling dropout prevention intervention: Some cautions on isolating at-risk adolescents within high schools. *American Education Research Journal, 24*(4), 521-540.

Chalfant, J. C., & Pysh, M. V. (1981, November). Teacher assistance teams: A model for within-building problem solving. *Counterpoint.* Reston, VA: Council for Exceptional Children.

Chalfant, J. C., & Pysh, M. V. (1989). *Teacher assistance teams: Five descriptive studies on 96 teams.* Manuscript submitted for publication.

Chalfant, J. C., Pysh, M. V., & Moultrie, R. (1979). Teacher assistance teams: A model for within-building problem solving. *Learning Disabilities Quarterly, 2,* 85-95.

Chalker, C. (1990, February). *Reduction of secondary school students at risk: At-risk student identification, support services, and multidisciplinary group intervention.* Paper presented at the Southeastern Conference on At-Risk Students, Savannah, GA.

Edmonds, R. (1979). Some schools work and more can. *Social Policy, 9,* 28-32.

Friedman, R. M. (1986). Major issues in mental health services for children. *Administration in Mental Health, 14*(1), 6-13.

Friedman, R. M., & Stroul, B. A. (1988). Principles for a system of care. *Children Today, 17*(4), 11-15.

Frymier, J. (1989). The Phi Delta Kappa study of students at risk. *Phi Delta Kappan, 71*(2), 142-146.

Fuchs, D., & Fuchs, L. (1990). Mainstream assistance teams: A scientific basis for the art of consultation. *Exceptional Children, 57*(2), 128-139.

Garibaldi, A. M. (1978). *In-school alternatives to suspension: Report to National Institute of Education.* Washington, DC: National Institute of Education.

Glasser, W. (1969). *Schools without failure.* New York: Harper & Row.

Glickman, C. D., & Tamashiro, R. T. (1980). Clarifying teachers' beliefs about discipline. *Educational Leadership, 37,* 459-464.

Good, T., & Brophy, J. (1984). *Looking in classrooms.* New York: Harper & Row.

Gottredson, D. (1984, August). *Environmental change strategies to prevent school disruption.* Paper presented at the annual meeting of the American Psychological Association, Toronto, Canada.

Graden, J. L., Casey, A., & Bonstrom, O. (1985). Implementing a prereferral intervention system: Part II. The data. *Exceptional Children, 51,* 487-496.

Graden, J. L., Casey, A., & Christenson, S. L. (1985). Implementing a prereferral intervention system: Part I. The model. *Exceptional Children, 51,* 377-387.

Gregory, T., & Smith, G. R. (1983, April). *Differences between alternative and conventional school in meeting students' needs.* Paper presented at the annual meeting of the American Educational Research Association, Montreal, Canada.

Guilford, J. P. (1977). *Way beyond the I.Q.* Buffalo, NY: Creative Educational Foundation, Inc.

Harrington, R. G., & Gibson, E. (1986). Preassessment procedures for learning disabled children: Are they effective? *Journal of Learning Disabilities, 9,* 538-541.

Hayek, R. A. (1987). The teacher assistance team: A pre-referral support system. *Focus on Exceptional Children, 20*(1), 1-7.

Hrncir, E. J., & Eisenhart, C. E. (1991). Use with caution: The "at-risk" label. *Young Children, 46*(2), 23-27.

Hurt, H. T., Scott, M. D., & McCroskey, J. C. (1978). *Communications in the classroom.* Reading, MA: Addison-Wesley.

Kirk, S. A. (1986). Redesigning delivery systems for learning disabled students. *Learning Disabilities Focus, 2*(1), 4-6.

Knitzer, J. (1984). Mental health services to children and adolescents: A national view of public policies. *American Psychologist, 39,* 905-911.

Kortz, W. H. (1986). *Student discipline.* Austin: Texas Public School Organization.

Kounin, J. S. (1970). *Discipline and group management in classrooms.* New York: Holt, Rinehart & Winston.

Krajewski, R. J. (1977, April). *Implications of a rank ordering process by elementary principals.* Paper presented at the annual meeting of the National Association of Elementary School Principals, Las Vegas, NV.

Leatt, D. J. (1987). In-school suspension programs for at-risk students. *OSSC Bulletin, 30*(7), 1-35.

Lloyd, J. W., Crowley, E. P., Kohler, F. W., & Strain, P. S. (1988). Redefining the applied research agenda: Cooperative learning, prereferral, teacher consultation, and peer-mediated interventions. *Journal of Learning Disabilities, 21*(1), 43-52.

Lordon, J. F. (1983). Establishing a climate for school discipline: A total perspective. *NASSP Bulletin, 67*(462), 58-60.

McCormick, K. (1989). *An equal chance: Educating at-risk children to succeed.* Alexandria, VA: National School Boards Association.

Mearig, J. S. (1982). Integration of school and community services for children with special needs. In C. R. Reynolds & T. B. Gutkin (Eds.), *Handbook of school psychology* (pp. 186-203). New York: John Wiley.

Mendez, R., & Sanders, S. G. (1981). An examination of in-school suspension: Panacea or Pandora's Box. *NASSP Bulletin, 65*(441), 65-69.

Metz, M. H. (1978). *Classrooms and corridors.* Berkeley: University of California Press.

Mizell, M. H. (1979). Designing and implementing effective in-school alternatives to suspension. In A. Garibaldi (Ed.), *In-school alternatives to suspension* (pp. 107-120). Washington, DC: Government Printing Office.

Moore, W. L., & Cooper, H. (1984). Correlations between teacher and student background and teacher perceptions of discipline problems and disciplinary techniques. *Psychology in the Schools, 21*, 386-392.

National Association of School Psychologists. (1986). *Intervention assistance teams: A model for building level instructional problem solving.* Stratford, CT: Author.

Ogden, E. H., & Germinario, V. (1988). *The at-risk student: Answers for educators.* Lancaster, PA: Technomic.

Pare, J. A. (1983). Alternative learning centers: Another option for discipline programs. *NASSP Bulletin, 67*(462), 61-67.

Phi Delta Kappan Center for Evaluation, Development, and Research. (1981, September). *Discipline: Practical applications of research, IV*(1).

Ponti, C., Zins, J., & Graden, J. L. (1988). Implementing a consultation-based service delivery system to decrease referrals for special education: A case study of organizational considerations. *School Psychology Review, 17,* 89-100.

Reale, F. (1966). *When we deal with children.* New York: Free Press.

Reed, R. J. (1983). Administrators' advice: Causes and remedies of school conflict and violence. *NASSP Bulletin, 67*(462), 75-79.

Rhodes, E. M. (1956). *A bar cross man: The life and personal writings of Eugene Manlove Rhodes.* Norman: University of Oklahoma Press.

Rich, K. M., & Heintzelman, G. K. (1989, March). *Development of district-wide intervention assistance teams.* Paper presented at the annual convention of the National Association of School Psychologists, Boston, MA.

Rubel, R. J. (1986). *Student discipline strategies: School system and police response to high risk and disruptive youth.* Paper presented at the Working Meeting on Student Discipline Strategies of Research, Office of Educational Research and Improvement, U.S. Department of Education, Washington, DC.

Saxe, L. E., Cross, T., & Silverman, N. (1988). Children's mental health: The gap between what we know and what we do. *American Psychologist, 43,* 800-807.

Short, P. M. (1988). Effectively disciplined schools: Three themes from research. *NASSP Bulletin, 72*(504), 1-3.

Short, P. M., & Clark, S. (1988). The effect of a school-wide discipline management program on school discipline. *Educational and Psychological Research, 8*(3), 203-212.

Short, P. M., & Noblit, G. W. (1985). Missing the mark in in-school suspension: An explanation and proposal. *NASSP Bulletin, 69*(484), 112-116.

Short, P. M., & Short, R. J. (1985a, October). *Organizational discipline: Critical factors in analyzing and planning discipline.* Paper presented at the annual conference of the International Society for Educational Planning, Kansas City, MO.

Short, P. M., & Short, R. J. (1985b, November). *Teacher philosophy, organizational climate, and discipline: The mix and the match.* Paper presented at the annual conference of the Texas Association for Supervision and Curriculum Development, Houston, TX.

Short, P. M., & Short, R. J. (1987). Beyond technique: Personal and organizational influences on school discipline. *The High School Journal, 71*(1), 31-36.

Short, P. M., & Short, R. J. (1988). Perceived classroom environment and student behavior in secondary schools. *Educational Research Quarterly, 12*(3), 35-39.

Short, R. J., Meadows, M. E., & Moracco, J. C. (1992). A project to meet the needs of rural at-risk children: Pilot At-Risk Interventions in Rural Schools (PAIRS). In R. C. Morris (Ed.), *Solving the problems of youth at risk: Involving parents and community resources* (pp. 176-180). Lancaster, PA: Technomic.

Short, R. J., & Short, P. M. (1990). Teacher beliefs, perceptions of behavior problems, and intervention preferences. *Journal of Social Studies Research, 13*(2), 28-33.

Short, R. J., & Talley, R. C. (1990). *The effect of teacher assistance teams on problem referrals in elementary schools.* Unpublished manuscript.

Sykora, R. J. (1981). In-school suspension—Alternatives within an option. *NASSP Bulletin, 65*(441), 119-122.

Ward, S. (1982). Student characteristics and precipitating events in relation to dropping out of high school (Doctoral dissertation, University of North Carolina, 1981). *Dissertation Abstracts International, 43,* 263A.

Wayson, W. (1985). The politics of violence in the schools: Doublespeak and disruptions in public confidence. *Phi Delta Kappan, 67*(2), 127-132.

Willower, D. J. (1975). Some comments on inquiries on schools and pupil control. *Teachers College Record, 77*(2), 221-230.

Willower, D. J., Eidell, T. L., & Hoy, W. K. (1967). *The school and pupil control ideology* (Monograph No. 24). University Park: Pennsylvania State University Studies.

Wolfgang, C. H., & Glickman, C. D. (1980). *Solving discipline problems: Strategies for classroom teachers.* Boston: Allyn & Bacon.

Wu, S., Pink, W., Crain, R., & Moles, O. (1982). Student suspension: A critical reappraisal. *Urban Review, 14*(4), 245-303.

Wynn, E. A. (1981). Looking at good schools. *Phi Delta Kappan, 62,* 377-381.

Yanossy, W. J. (1986). *An intervention program to reduce the number of discipline referrals of high-risk ninth-grade students.* Ft. Lauderdale, FL: NOVA University Center for the Advancement of Education.

Author Index

Subject Index